Praise for *The Longing in Me* and Sheila Walsh

"Sheila is a truth-teller, wise counsel, and a force of raw honesty in a harsh world that begs us to be perfect. This book sings of release: from unfair expectations, from my own self-condemnation, and into the arms of Jesus who has no notion of halfway love."

—Jen Hatmaker, *New York Times*
bestselling author of *For the Love*

"We share an ache in our hearts, an emptiness in our souls. It's an emptiness only God can fill—Sheila's book taught me that in new and beautiful ways. Now it's your turn."

—Karen Kingsbury, *New York Times*
bestselling author of numerous novels,
including *Brush of Wings*

"Sheila Walsh has the uncanny ability to plumb the deepest truths without sounding superficial or preachy. She touches the heart, soothes the soul, and lifts the spirit."

—Max Lucado, *New York Times* bestselling
author of *You'll Get Through This*

"Sheila meets us with the comfort of a treasured friend, willing to ask the questions that lie under the surface of our well-displayed selves."

—Jenni Catron, author of *The 4 Dimensions
of Extraordinary Leadership* and *Clout*

"To sit under [Sheila's] ministry is to come nearer to the heart of God. Sheila is the genuine article and I am confident that all who draw near to her story, experience, and wisdom will be forever changed."

—Bobbie Houston, cofounder and senior
pastor of the Hillsong Church in
Sydney, Australia

"Sheila has an amazing ability to communicate the freedom and joy that are yours in Jesus, no matter who you are or what you might have gone through in life."

—Judah Smith, New York Times
bestselling author of Jesus Is _____
and Life Is _____

THE
LONGING
IN ME

ALSO BY SHEILA WALSH

NONFICTION

Loved Back to Life

The Storm Inside

God Loves Broken People

The Shelter of God's Promises

*Beautiful Things Happen When
a Woman Trusts God*

Get Off Your Knees and Pray

God Has a Dream for Your Life

Let Go

All That Really Matters

Extraordinary Faith

*I'm Not Wonder Woman but
God Made Me Wonderful*

A Love So Big

Living Fearlessly

Stones from the River of Mercy

The Heartache No One Sees

Life Is Tough but God Is Faithful

Gifts for Your Soul

Honestly

Bring Back the Joy

The Best Devotions of Sheila Walsh

Sparks in the Dark

CHILDREN'S BOOKS

You Are Worth It

You Are Worth It for Girls

Hello, Sun!

Hello, Stars!

Meet My Best Friend series

God's Little Princess series

God's Mighty Warrior series

The Gnoo Zoo series

GIFT BOOKS

*5 Minutes with Jesus,
Make Today Matter*

5 Minutes with Jesus, Peace for Today

God's Shelter in Your Storm

Outrageous Love

Come as You Are

Good Morning, Lord

BIBLE STUDY CURRICULUM

The Longing in Me

The Storm Inside

The Shelter of God's Promises

FICTION

Angel Song (with Kathryn Cushman)

Sweet Sanctuary (with
Cindy Martinsen)

Song of the Brokenhearted
(with Cindy Martinsen)

THE
LONGING
IN ME

How Everything You Crave
Leads *to the* Heart *of* God

SHEILA
WALSH

NELSON
BOOKS

An Imprint of Thomas Nelson

Published in Nashville, Tennessee, by Nelson Books, an imprint of Thomas Nelson. Nelson Books and Thomas Nelson are registered trademarks of HarperCollins Christian Publishing, Inc.

Author is represented by the literary agency of Alive Communications, Inc., 7680 Goddard Street, Suite 200, Colorado Springs, CO 80902, www.alivecommunications.com.

Thomas Nelson titles may be purchased in bulk for educational, business, fund-raising, or sales promotional use. For information, please e-mail SpecialMarkets@ThomasNelson.com.

In some instances, names, dates, locations, and other identifying details have been changed to protect the identities and privacy of those mentioned in this book.

Unless otherwise indicated Scripture quotations are taken from the *Holy Bible*, New Living Translation. © 1996, 2004, 2007, 2013 by Tyndale House Foundation. Used by permission of Tyndale House Publishers, Inc., Carol Stream, Illinois 60188. All rights reserved.

Scripture quotations marked AMP are from the Amplified® Bible. Copyright © 1954, 1958, 1962, 1964, 1965, 1987 by The Lockman Foundation. Used by permission. (www.Lockman.org)

Scripture quotations marked KJV are from the King James Version. Public domain.

Scripture quotations marked THE MESSAGE are from *The Message*. Copyright © by Eugene H. Peterson 1993, 1994, 1995, 1996, 2000, 2001, 2002. Used by permission of Tyndale House Publishers, Inc.

Scripture quotations marked NASB are from New American Standard Bible®. Copyright © 1960, 1962, 1963, 1968, 1971, 1972, 1973, 1975, 1977, 1995 by The Lockman Foundation. Used by permission. (www.Lockman.org)

Scripture quotations marked NIV are from the Holy Bible, New International Version®, NIV®. Copyright © 1973, 1978, 1984, 2011 by Biblica, Inc.® Used by permission of Zondervan. All rights reserved worldwide. www.zondervan.com. The 'NIV and 'New International Version are trademarks registered in the United States Patent and Trademark Office by Biblica, Inc.®

ISBN 978-0718079529 (IE)

Library of Congress Cataloging-in-Publication Data

Names: Walsh, Sheila, 1956-
Title: The longing in me : how everything you crave leads to the heart of God / Sheila Walsh.
Description: Nashville : Thomas Nelson, 2016. | Includes bibliographical references.
Identifiers: LCCN 2015034686 | ISBN 9781400204892
Subjects: LCSH: Emotions--Religious aspects--Christianity. |
  Desire--Religious aspects--Christianity. | Desire for God.
Classification: LCC BV4597.3 .W35 2016 | DDC 248.4--dc23
LC record available at http://lccn.loc.gov/2015034686

Printed in the United States of America

16 17 18 19 20   RRD   10 9 8 7 6 5 4 3 2 1

This book is dedicated in memory of my friend and book agent, Lee Hough, no longer longing but finally home.

The books or the music in which we thought the beauty was located will betray us if we trust to them; it was not in them, it only came through them, and what came through was a longing. These things—the beauty, the memory of our own past—are good images of what we really desire; but if they are mistaken for the thing itself they turn into dumb idols, breaking the hearts of their worshippers.

For they are not the thing itself; they are only the scent of a flower we have not found, the echo of a tune we have not heard, news from a country we have never yet visited.[1]

—C. S. Lewis, *The Weight of Glory*

CONTENTS

INTRODUCTION

> It seems to me we can never give up longing
> and wishing while we are thoroughly alive.
> There are certain things we feel to be beautiful
> and good, and we *must* hunger after them.[1]
> —*George Eliot*

IT GREW DARK AS WE PULLED ONTO THE A74, the road that connects the west coast of Scotland to England's Lake District. It was raining quite hard, so my husband of six hours sat quietly, concentrating on the road ahead. I was quiet too. I had a terrible sense of foreboding, not what you would expect on the evening of your wedding day. Even so, I didn't see the accident coming.

All I remember now is the terrifying sound of screeching brakes and then the sickening noise of one car smashing into another, then another, metal twisting like pipe cleaners, broken glass flying through the air, caught in the headlights of oncoming traffic. Then for a moment . . . silence.

Once my husband was sure I wasn't seriously hurt, he got out of the car to see what had happened. We were number six in a ten-car pileup. The man who had smashed into the back of our car came to the passenger side and opened my door.

"You need to get out," he said, wiping a small stream of blood that had erupted from a gash in his forehead. "Some of these cars could catch fire."

My right knee was bleeding where it had banged into something on the dashboard, and I had a cut on the right side of my head that dripped blood down over my ear and onto my collar. I grabbed my scarf and pressed it against the cut as I undid my seat belt and got out. Oncoming traffic had stopped. In the glare of headlights, I saw a woman lying on the side of the road, a man bent over her, calling her name. I didn't know whether she had been struck crossing the road or if she had been thrown from her car. The first two cars were almost unrecognizable; the second was the worst. The whole front end was crushed and twisted. The driver slumped over the wheel. Everything about his body angle was wrong. Someone sobbed in the back of his car. I heard a woman in the rapidly growing crowd of onlookers say that she was a doctor, so I moved out of the way.

I had no idea where we were. Were we still in Scotland, or had we crossed the border into England? I looked around, trying to get my bearings. All I could see on either side of the road were fields. I sat down on the wet grass, my "going-away" outfit already bloody and ruined. In the distance flashing blue lights came closer and closer, sirens blaring. I looked at our car, crumpled in the front and back, certainly not drivable.

In that moment, the strangest thing happened. I heard myself say out loud, "This is a picture of your life now, Sheila. You fought everyone to be able to marry this man, and now it's done and no one cares anymore. You are on your own."

I had no idea that night just how true those words would prove to be.

During the last thirty years since that bloody night, I've written a lot of books, but I've never talked about my first marriage. Partly because one person can never give an accurate account of two lives and partly because there were so many painful moments that have taken time to begin to process and understand.

In December 2012, my ex-husband died. For the first time I feel that I can tell this part of my story, not to harm his memory in any way, not at all, but simply to own my part of that journey and the lessons Christ continues to teach me today along this twisted road we all travel.

In "Little Gidding," the last of the four poems in T. S. Eliot's *Four Quartets*, he wrote:

> *We shall not cease from exploration*
> *And the end of all our exploring*
> *Will be to arrive where we started*
> *And know the place for the first time.*[2]

I love this quote. I have written it down over and over again through the years because it resonates so deeply inside me.

Does it connect with you?

Let me ask you this. Do you ever feel as if you keep coming back to the same place in life over and over again and you wonder why you're here? Didn't you learn all you had to learn the last time?

You vowed you'd never repeat the same mistakes, react in the same way, and yet here you find yourself, right back smack in the middle of it all one more time!

What I'm learning is that if I don't understand why I respond a certain way in a particular set of circumstances, I'll do it again and again. The human heart longs for closure and understanding. In many ways it longs to right the wrongs of our childhood so we feel more in control of situations over which we had no control as children. We try to change the ending of something that scarred us badly. My prayer in this book is to help you find the one true Source who can meet your deepest longings so you can change the way you respond to life's stresses, to give you real tools to heal from the past and find joy today.

When I looked for a companion to take along on this trip with us, there was no one finer than King David, the greatest king that Israel ever had. He was known as "a man after God's own heart" (see 1 Sam. 13:14; Acts

13:22), and yet he made some of the worst choices, ones that cost him and others dearly. As we walk through David's life, my life, and the lives of other women, we'll study the longings we all have and learn how to channel those to know God more and determine what to do when we lose our way. Longings are a part of life. They are not inherently good or evil.

A baby comes into the world with very primal longings:

To be held
To be fed
To sleep
To be clean and dry

Babies don't wonder if it's a good time for their mom to respond or if it's in the middle of the night; they simply roar out their need until they are heard. The longings continue into our adult lives.

We long to be seen.
We long to be chosen.
We long to be loved.
We long to know that we matter.

When those longings are left unmet, what do we do? Where do we go?

Perhaps even more confusing, when those longings are met, why is there an even greater ache that remains?

I believe it is a sacred ache, a longing for the very heart of God.

I feel I should show my hand a little here and let you into a secret I discovered that has changed—and continues to change—everything in my life, moment by moment. It helps me understand my past, fully engage in my present, and find hope for the future. It's a staggering, hard-to-grasp, will-rock-your-world truth: no matter how great your longing is for God, it will never, ever compare to His longing for you!

My prayer for you right now, dear reader, is that God will grant you the grace and courage to pursue Him and, along that broken path, discover how much God has always loved and relentlessly pursued you.

ONE

The Longing to Be Chosen

Fully, 100 percent chosen and fully, 100 percent
known. Every good and bad thing . . . known!
It didn't keep Him from giving His all for us,
and He still keeps giving. Many can't know the
power of this sacred privilege until they struggle
enough in life to understand their need for it.[1]
—*Mike Colaw*

You didn't choose me. I chose you. I appointed
you to go and produce lasting fruit, so that the
Father will give you whatever you ask for, using my
name. This is my command: Love each other.
—*John 15:16–17*

HE WAS A LAB TECHNICIAN IN THE PHYSICS
department in my high school. I don't remember his name but I remember his face because I dreamed about him at night. He had long, dark hair that grazed the collar of his white lab coat, big brown eyes, and just enough of a beard to cast him in my fertile imagination as a man of mystery. He wasn't particularly tall, five feet ten or eleven inches, but I decided that God had packed a lot into every single masculine inch.

Part of me knew he was out of my league. He was, after all, technically "staff," and I was an awkward high school senior. I had greasy hair and chin acne that I tried to cover up with "flesh colored" Clearasil (which I'm sure would have done the trick had you been unfortunate enough to be born with an orange chin).

Even so I dared to dream. I would imagine I was walking along the school corridor, carrying my books, and *he* would bump into me, knocking me over and sending my books in all directions. He would, of course, apologize profusely as he bent to pick them up. Our eyes would meet. He would hold my gaze for a few seconds more than normal, and even as my face flushed an attractive, feminine shade of pink, he would take my hand and help me to my feet.

"Will you be at the senior dance this weekend?" he would inquire.

"I will," I would reply, a slight tremor in my voice, which I decided men found attractive.

"Will you save a dance for me?" he would ask.

This is where I got a bit stuck. Should I reply, "I'll save them all for you!" or, "I will try to save you one"? I didn't want to sound desperate or too available or uninterested. There is nothing about being raised as a Scottish Baptist that prepares a girl for the ways of love.

For the three remaining days before the dance, I walked past his lab, laden with books, so many times that I had to get two aspirin from the school nurse for the pain in my shoulders . . . but all to no avail. He failed to make an appearance, much less an encounter.

I didn't even know if he would be at the senior dance until I overheard Laura (name changed for obvious reasons) mention his name while I waited in line for the school bus. Laura was beautiful. She had long, silky, chestnut hair; sultry brown eyes; and a spectacularly flawless chin. Laura and I were in several classes together, but I don't think she even knew my name. I wasn't part of the beautiful crowd who revered her as their leader. I could only catch snippets of the bus-line conversation, but

I heard enough to know that "he" was going to be at the senior dance. Foolishly I blurted out, "That's so great!"

Laura and two of her friends turned around to see who had punctured the golden bubble of their conversation with such an uncouth outburst.

"Sorry!" I said. "I just think he's a great lab technician, and that must be tiring, and it must be nice to get out." With every pathetic word that staggered out of my mouth and over my spotty chin, the girls pulled slightly farther away. Mercifully, deliverance came in the form of the school bus, which roared slightly louder than I had.

On the night of the dance, I anticipated the beginning of the more romantic stage of my life; I was dressed and ready three hours before I needed to leave. I didn't know what to do with myself, so I just paced around the living room until my mom begged me to stop before she had to replace the carpet. Finally the time arrived, and my friend Moira's dad pulled up in his car to transport the two of us to the school hall.

The social committee had done a fantastic job transforming the room where we sat every morning for assembly into a fancy nightclub with flashing lights and the requisite disco ball. The first few songs were fast, and most of the students danced together with no particular partner. But then a slow song began. Those who weren't dating cleared the floor, leaving nine or ten couples under the lights. I retreated to a corner and pressed my back against the wall, feeling a familiar loneliness creep over me, a feeling I had known since my father's suicide when I was a child. I was five when he drowned himself, and part of me had been drowning ever since.

I looked around the room to find Moira. Instead I saw *him* walking toward me. I looked to see who was standing beside me. Was it Laura or one of her girls? But they stood together on the other side of the hall, and they were watching him getting closer and closer to me. My heart pounded out of my chest as he walked right up to me and asked, "Do you want to dance?"

I don't think I even replied. I just took his outstretched hand as he led me to the dance floor. I remember the song that was playing, "A Whiter Shade of Pale," an older song by Procol Harum. I knew all the words. Simply perfect. I rested my head on his shoulder as we danced. I pulled back and looked into his eyes.

That's when everything changed.

He said, "I'm so sorry. I can't do this."

He let go of me and walked over to where Laura and her friends clumped together, laughing. It had clearly been a dare, a bet, a why-don't-you-dance-with-the-awkward-girl?

I thought of going all "Carrie" on them, but I just slipped away and hid in the girls' restroom until Moira found me when her dad arrived to take us home.

Even now, all these years later, I can still remember that sickening feeling in the pit of my stomach. I felt so stupid, and I was angry. I was angry with Laura, I was angry with her friends, I was angry with the lab technician (who I saw at close range, by the way, had grown a beard to cover up *his* chin acne!), but most of all I was angry with myself.

Why did I imagine for one moment that someone that attractive would choose me?

Why had I let them make a fool of me?

Why had I set myself up to be hurt one more time?

I disgusted myself, and I felt deeply, profoundly alone.

Have you ever felt that way?

You dared to dream for just a moment that you would get chosen, only to be disappointed one more time, and now you have to remind yourself that you will never be "that girl."

I've often wondered if that's why little girls love fairy tales. Is it because they always have a happy ending?

Do we love them because the girl we identify with gets picked, even if she's the least likely one, the one who is made to sweep up cinders while her ugly, mean sisters get ready for the ball, and yet she gets chosen in the end? Or because, after the story takes a disastrous turn and she takes a bite of the poisoned apple, just as all seems lost, the prince arrives and saves her? The credits roll. In our vivid imaginations, they live a perfect life.

These are the stories of our childhood, but it seems today we need a story to take us beyond our childhood into young adulthood.

In 2005 American author Stephenie Meyer published the first of four books in her fantasy romance series about vampires and werewolves. The story's heroine is a very ordinary girl named Bella Swan, who falls in love with Edward Cullen, a 104-year-old vampire. The series sold more than 120 million copies and has been translated into thirty-eight languages. In 2008 the last of the four, *Breaking Dawn*, won the British Book Award for Children's Book of the Year, and the following year the series as a whole won Kids' Choice Award for Favorite Book.[2]

Think about that for a moment. A series of books about an ordinary girl being pursued by both a vampire and a werewolf captivated instead of terrified the hearts and minds of millions of children and young women around the world. Why?

Was it because Edward was aware of her every move, because he watched over her day and night and knew if she was in any danger at all? Was it because out of all the girls he had ever met during 104 years of being undead (think about it; that's a lot of girls), he chose her?

Whatever the reason, it resonated deeply and tapped into the longing of every girl's heart, that longing to be singled out and chosen.

Whether it's Bella from *Twilight* or Cinderella, deep inside we long to be seen and known, loved and chosen. If that were the story we actually lived, we'd have no need for fairy tales or vampire sagas because readers would have no gaping holes to fill with fairy tales.

Now, I'm not suggesting that every little girl who loves to dress up as her favorite Disney princess is trying to fill an empty void. That's just part of the fantasy fun of childhood. Those childish tales can simply be part of the normal stuff of life. But for some of us, these stories highlight and deepen the longing in a broken heart. When we've had a happy childhood and been well parented, our internal radar looks for those admirable qualities in a mate. We want someone with good boundaries and fairly healthy self-esteem, someone who can handle a budget, who respects others and will respect us.

Many of us who were deeply wounded in childhood, however, have a warped picture of what that connectedness should look like. The innate longing to be loved and chosen can lead us into very damaging situations. We simply don't have a clear picture of what "normal" is. This warped perspective can lead us down many different heartbreaking roads.

I've read that sexual predators can sense when a young girl is broken and starving for affection, almost as if she emits a radar signal that she's looking for love and acceptance—and will take it in any form when "love" is offered.

The longing to be chosen is profoundly primal. When a young girl has a healthy relationship with her father, when she knows that she is loved and treasured, then that instinctive longing takes its place with every other desire and need in life. It weighs what it should. But when that need is unmet in childhood, the longing to be chosen becomes the driving force in life. As a young girl, I felt uncovered, exposed, un-protected. It was the perfect prelude to desperate choices.

―∞∞―

I had just finished leading worship with Graham Kendrick and his band on the main stage of Britain's largest Christian arts festival, Greenbelt. It was an unusually hot, sticky August day. Some friends and I made our way across the vast field that housed the stage at one end, the concession stands at the other. We needed something cold to drink in a bad way.

Suddenly I heard the noise of a car engine and thought, *What idiot is driving across the field?*

It soon became plain as the car pulled up right beside us. The driver looked at me and said, "Can I talk to you for a minute?"

I looked around. Was he speaking to me?

He laughed, then got out of the car, stepping onto the muddied field. I noted his wing tips. The man extended his hand, introduced himself—I'll call him John—and added, "I'm a record executive." And he mentioned a few of the artists he worked with.

Now I listened.

"You have a great voice," he said.

I could feel my face getting hot. "Thank you," I said, noting his Scottish accent.

He returned to his car, mud-shoed.

I ran to catch up with my friends.

"Who was the guy in the red car?" one of them asked.

"Someone with more money than sense!" I said. "Imagine driving a car like that across a muddy field like this!"

I didn't meet him again for several weeks during my very first solo concert—something that terrified me. Graham Kendrick, best known for writing powerful worship songs, was my boss at British Youth for Christ. He had written some songs specifically for me. I'd been much more comfortable in the only role I knew, as a backup singer, but Graham encouraged me to step out and see how God might use me under the spotlight. My debut concert took place at a holiday camp in England that we'd taken over for a couple of weeks each year in the fall to host a very conservative Christian convention. Being a staff member at Youth for Christ, I was seen as safe and was brought in to "entertain the youth." I had great doubts as to how entertaining I would be, but the evening proved to be a life-changing event in many ways.

The concert hall quickly filled up as rumors of a band (as opposed to the usual one acoustic guitar and a tambourine) spread like wildfire. The band turned out to be great. I loved the songs Graham wrote. I surprised myself by loving every single minute of it. By the final song the crowd stood on their feet, yelling and clapping for more. It was both exhilarating and exhausting. That night I felt a deep sense of purpose. I had finally found a vehicle to communicate the love of God in a way that made sense to me. I thought of all the evenings I had walked along the beach, singing out to God, telling Him about my pain and my questions, yet deeply overwhelmed by His fiery, relentless love. Now I could sing that truth out loud to others. Wonderful.

As I left the stage that evening, the man with the red sports car and no sense stood nearby.

"You were amazing," he said.

"I was?"

He stepped closer. "I want to sign you to my record label."

"Well, that would be hard. I'm with Youth for Christ, so I can't do that."

Instead of hearing what I'd tried to communicate, he said, "I can make things happen."

I had a strong conviction that he was right.

When I finally got back to my little cabin that night, I replayed the events of the evening in my head—heady stuff for a girl like me. I'd never been chosen for anything, but tonight the crowd had voted and cast their ballot for the least likely one of all. Me.

Sound familiar? That seems to be God's way as well.

Remember, dear brothers and sisters, that few of you were wise in the world's eyes or powerful or wealthy when God called you. Instead, God chose things the world considers foolish in order to shame those who think they are wise. And he chose things that are powerless to shame those who are powerful. God chose things despised by the world, things counted as nothing at all, and used them to bring to nothing what the world considers important. (1 Cor. 1:26–28)

I often wonder how seriously we take that passage in the church. We tend to look to the most articulate and gifted among us, but God has a different set of scales that He uses to measure a life. He looks at the heart. If you just take the last two lines of the passage above—"God chose things despised by the world, things counted as nothing at all, and used them to bring to nothing what the world considers important"—it reads exactly like the story of the life of David, the shepherd boy whom God chose to be king over Israel.

Nothing about his early days would have made anyone believe he would be the chosen one. His own father missed it, but then again, so did Samuel, God's prophet.

Before we meet David in Scripture, we're given a picture of what happens when God's people think they know what they need more than God does—a slippery slope.

Have you ever done that? Have you ever prayed a prayer and then been profoundly grateful in retrospect that God didn't answer it the way you asked Him to?

I know I have.

David wasn't the first king or the people's choice. He wasn't the one they wanted. You can read the whole story in 1 Samuel 8–10, but let me give you the "CliffsNotes" version.

Before Israel had a king, judges ruled them—some good, some not so good. Samuel was the last of the judges. He was an old man when the elders of Israel came to his home in Ramah. They had come for an intervention of sorts. Here's why. As Samuel aged, he had continued as judge in Ramah and the nearby towns, but he had appointed his two deadbeat sons as judges on the southern border of Israel. Whether he should have done that or not is questionable because we're told throughout the book of Judges that God appointed a new judge. Add to that the fact that his sons took bribes and twisted justice and you get a bit of a picture of the mess that led up to this meeting with Samuel. The elders put their cards on the table:

" 'Look,' they told him, 'you are now old, and your sons are not like you. Give us a king to judge us like all the other nations have' " (1 Sam. 8:5).

Pretty sad three-pronged statement when you think about it:

1. You're too old.
2. Your sons are hopeless.
3. We want to be like other nations.

Israel, God's chosen people, wanted to be just like everyone else. Samuel was devastated that the people showed such faithlessness. Not only that, but he carried the heartache of seeing his own children reject everything he had ever taught them.

Some of you might be there right now. How the enemy loves to torture parents who have been faithful but whose children appear faithless. Our son, Christian, is about to go off to college as I write this, and he is a great boy, but I know there will be moments in life when I will need to resist the torments of the enemy and stand on the truth that our God is sovereign and my son is on His schedule, not mine. Nothing will happen to your child today or tomorrow that doesn't pass through the merciful hands of God, even though at times it will feel like a severe, tearstained mercy.

There are many lessons for us to learn from the faithlessness of God's people. The children of Israel demanded a king, but they already had a King. They always had a divine King in God. Now they wanted what made sense to them, what they could see with their eyes.

I wonder if I'm much different at times.

God's Word is filled with more than three thousand promises. But when I walk through a hard season, I want tangible signs that God is going to come through for me.

Do you ever find yourself there?

We long for love and acceptance. We know that God loves us, but we can't see God with our eyes or feel His arms around us or hear His audible voice telling us that we are loved. So we look for that kind of love and acceptance in someone else.

If I could step back in time and talk to myself as I stood embarrassed under a disco ball, or caught up with myself running over that muddy field, or interrupt the high after my first concert, I would have said, "Sheila you are chosen. You're chosen by the One who will never unchoose you. You're loved when the crowd cheers and when the lights go out and they all go home."

But we don't get to do that, do we? As T. S. Eliot wrote, we just keep finding ourselves back at the same place again with a little more understanding.

So, back to the children of Israel. God said to Samuel, "If that's what the people want, let them have their king."

As they looked around, the Israelites saw that every other nation had a king who was a strong warrior leader, who would take them into battle. They wanted a victorious warrior-king too. Not only that, they wanted a king who looked like a king. That's exactly what they got in Saul. He was tall, dark, and handsome, but on that day when the people cried out, "Long live the king!" they had no idea what they had just signed up for.

Saul started well, but before long he showed how flawed his character really was. Life is like that. We can all put on a good face for a time, but add enough pressure and stress, and our wounds and flaws will surface. Israel's king showed himself to be a mean, selfish, petty, and violent man. But in God's eyes, he was a law unto himself. Three times Samuel caught him in serious acts of disobedience to God.

✳ He offered a sacrifice that he had no right to offer. He had been instructed to wait for Samuel. (See 1 Sam. 13.)

✳ He made the men in his care take a rash vow that almost cost him the life of his own son Jonathan. (See 1 Sam. 14.)

✳ He directly disobeyed a specific instruction from God to kill King Agag. This final act of defiance cost him everything and led to these tragic words: "And the LORD regretted that he had made Saul king over Israel" (1 Sam. 15:35 ESV).

Saul's disobedience broke Samuel's heart. He grieved so hard and so long that God finally intervened and said, "Enough!" It must have seemed to Samuel that everything had gone wrong. But he would live to see that no matter how often we fail God, God never fails us.

We are introduced to David in person in 1 Samuel 16 but meet his character before that. In the last conversation Samuel ever had with Saul, he said this: "But now your kingdom must end, for the LORD has sought out a man after his own heart" (1 Sam. 13:14).

What an incredible commendation from God, a letter of reference from the Most High. I can't think of anything I want more in life than that—to be known as a woman after God's own heart!

God instructed Samuel to go to Bethlehem, where He had already chosen a king from Jesse's sons. Do you remember who Jesse was? He was Ruth and Boaz's grandson. Ruth's story is the antithesis of the children of Israel's. She wasn't born an Israelite. She married into the nation. Then, even after her husband died, she refused to abandon her mother-in-law. Instead, she traveled with her to Bethlehem, saying, "Your people will be my people and your God will be my God" (Ruth 1:16). That passionate faithfulness had trickled down through the years and would also be found in a teenage boy out watching his father's sheep.

This is what God told Samuel to do:

"Take a heifer with you . . . and say that you have come to make a sacrifice to the LORD. Invite Jesse to the sacrifice, and I will show you which of his sons to anoint for me." So Samuel did as the LORD instructed.

When he arrived at Bethlehem, the elders of the town came trembling to meet him.

These were days when it was alarming for people to see God's prophet show up in town. According to author and professor G. Frederick Owen, "The people were on a long drift from God."[3] But word was out that the king they had chosen had turned crazy. Now here stood God's mouthpiece, having shown up uninvited.

"What's wrong?" they asked. "Do you come in peace?"

"Yes," Samuel replied. "I have come to sacrifice to the LORD. Purify yourselves and come with me to the sacrifice." Then Samuel performed the purification rite for Jesse and his sons and invited them to the sacrifice, too.

When they arrived, Samuel took one look at Eliab and thought, "Surely this is the LORD's anointed!" But the LORD said to Samuel, "Don't judge by his appearance or height, for I have rejected him. The LORD doesn't see things the way you see them. People judge by outward appearance, but the LORD looks at the heart." (1 Sam. 16:2–7)

Though the minute Samuel saw Jesse's oldest son, he knew he'd found his man, God said no. Eliab was the one everyone would have chosen—the eldest, strong, handsome—but God told Samuel that he'd already rejected him. He didn't pass heart inspection.

Next, Jesse offered up the other six sons he'd brought with him, and each time God said no.

Finally Samuel asked if this was it, or if there were any others.

"There is still the youngest," Jesse replied. "But he's out in the fields watching the sheep and goats" (v. 11).

Isn't it interesting that Jesse didn't think it was worth bringing David out? After all, who was he? He was just a kid watching the flocks. Yet while he shepherded in silence, God saw him.

Now, let me ask you: How many ministry opportunities do you think David had out in the field? None that we would have noticed, but God did not miss one. He heard the psalms that David sang over the flock. He saw his courage as David risked his own life to snatch a lamb from the paw of a bear or a young goat from a lion. He discerned David's heart and knew that this teenage boy who would sing in the darkness and fight in the light would be the one He would anoint as king of Israel.

I hope that encourages you as it does me. If you tend to look at other women and compare yourself to them, this story should be a wake-up call. Even within the church and parachurch organizations, we often discern wrongly. We're drawn by charisma more than by character. But charisma cracks under pressure while character doesn't.

David never asked to be chosen. He'd been hidden away, serving God with a full heart, when God's choice ran like oil over his head. I, on the other hand, had a desperate need to be seen and chosen. When need is in the driver's seat, you can find yourself on the side of the road in the rain with the smell of smoke all around you. Like me, and like a lady I'll call Mary.

I never found out what her real name was, but I identified with her story. We were sitting opposite each other, waiting to board a flight. I asked her if she'd watch my bag while I went to get a bottle of water, and when I got back, she'd moved to sit beside me.

"I've read one of your books," she said. "I think we have some things in common."

She told me that her dad was a good man but he was always busy when she was growing up, there but not really there. "Even when we had special dates, he'd miss them," she said. "There was always a good reason, so I couldn't ever get mad. I guess I just got used to it."

She told me that through high school and college she had longed to find someone who was different, but kept choosing guys who never kept their word. "You'd think I would have known better," she said. "I always felt that I wasn't pretty enough or thin enough. I just wasn't enough."

At that point the airline began to board our flight, and we never got to finish our conversation. By the time we landed and I made my way to baggage claim, she was gone. I prayed for Mary a lot that day. I prayed she would know that God keeps every appointment with His daughters, even when we forget.

Have you ever found yourself in a place like Mary's?

Have your longings ever landed you right in it?

Do you ever find yourself thinking that nothing will ever change?

I want to pause here and acknowledge how painful that is, but I don't want to leave you there. As a daughter of the Most High God, everything can change! It just takes some time and some commitment to begin thinking a new way.

Here, at the end of this chapter, I want you to do something for me. Why don't you find a three-by-five card and write on it:

> The God who created me has chosen me as
> His beautifully loved daughter. Because of
> that I can take other rejections in stride.

Now, place it somewhere that you'll see it every day, and read it over and over until you begin to believe it more than the lie that you are not worthy of being chosen. The God of the universe has already chosen you and says to you, "You are Mine!"

TWO

The Longing to Be Protected

I cannot think of any need in childhood as
strong as the need for a father's protection.[1]
—*Sigmund Freud*

The LORD is my light and my salvation—
so why should I be afraid?
The LORD is my fortress, protecting me from danger,
so why should I tremble?
—*Psalm 27:1*

BEFORE MY FATHER'S BRAIN INJURY, I WAS
fearless. I would climb trees and never think of falling; I would only see
the sky. But after his injury nothing felt safe. My final encounter with
him etched two messages into the tender tissue of my heart:

No one is going to protect you.
If you try to protect yourself, everyone will end up paying.

Was I aware of those new life rules? Absolutely not. But children
make life-altering vows that carry into adulthood, especially when they
feel they have failed those they love. I lived my life out of that punishing
place. Because of my father.

For some children this kind of soul damage takes place over time, like the endless drip, drip, drip of a faucet, wearing away the porcelain surface underneath. For others it's as if a bomb has been dropped on their lives, defacing the entire landscape. That's how it was for my family.

My dad had been hospitalized after his massive brain aneurism, but the doctors allowed him to come home and continue treatment with speech and physical therapy. During the next few days and weeks, his personality began to change. He would get very angry and strike out impulsively, and after that, even worse, he would weep. No one in the circle of those who loved him wanted to say whether it was safe to have dad at home. So at five years old, I made that decision for everyone.

I was sitting by the fire, playing with my wiener dog, Heidi, when she suddenly started to growl. I'd never heard her growl before, so I turned to see what she was growling at. In that horrifying second, I saw that my dad was about to bring his cane down on my skull. He looked like a giant hovering over me. I don't remember if I pulled on the cane or pushed it away from me, but he fell hard and lay roaring on the living room carpet. I had no idea in that moment that in defending myself I had just toppled the whole house down on all of us. Nothing was ever the same again. Dad ended up in the locked ward of an asylum, Mum lost her husband, and I stripped my sister and brother of a father. A lifetime is too short to pay for that kind of collateral damage.

Sometime after being institutionalized, my dad managed to escape one night. He then took his own life, drowning in the river that ran behind the hospital.

My sister, my brother, and I were too young to attend the funeral. And after that, we rarely talked about my dad. We certainly never talked about what happened that day. Even now we can't speak easily about these things as a family.

We know so much more today about how to help children process trauma and grief. Back then I'm sure my mum thought, *If Sheila wants to talk, she will.* She had no way of knowing the agonizing, shame-filled tapes that played over and over in my head.

At some point—I don't know when—I simply decided I must never make waves again. I would be a "good girl" and toe the party line, whatever party that might be. I vowed to never fell another giant.

I meet women like me all the time, usually in the church, because that's where we "good girls" go. We go because we love God and desperately want to believe God loves us. We go back because we are broken and the truth leaks out. I often think it would be helpful if those of us who have been dropped and broken as children had a little tattoo that was only visible to others who share that familiar story. We could find each other, commiserate, tell stories, and heal. But we don't have these identifying marks, so most of us feel as if we are completely alone. I read these letters of loneliness every day, and I weep with you because you are so much more beautiful and more valuable and stronger than you believe.

A girl who was sexually violated carries a burden she was not designed to carry. It's too heavy, too adult for someone who should be deciding if she wants to wear these shoes or those shoes. Once that sacred boundary has been crossed, there is no going back, no un-knowing what she has been forced to make space for. As she moves into young adulthood, it's hard to separate love from sex. Relationship after relationship takes a little piece of her soul. When "good" love does find her, how can she mix the rags from her past with the pristine white dress her future offers?

The girl whose father is there, but not there, will do anything to grab hold of his attention. The message that is penned onto her heart is that she is not pretty enough, not smart enough, not funny enough. She's simply *not enough.* She will often gravitate toward emotionally unavailable men because they are sickeningly familiar to her.

The woman who grew up in the foul-smelling shadow of alcoholism sits with her head in her hands in her bedroom late at night after her drunken husband has fallen asleep and asks herself, *Why? What is wrong with me that I chose this?*

The list could go on and on.

I pause for a moment here and pray for you. I don't know who you are or what your story is, but God does, and He loves you with a spectacularly brilliant, healing love. Even as you read these words, I wonder if you refuse to let them in. Some of the weightiest questions I am ever asked are why and where.

* "If God loves me so much, *where* was He when I was raped?"
* "If God loves me so much, *why* did my child die?"
* "If God loves me so much, *why* didn't He stop what was being done to me?"

I have no answers. Nothing. I could trot out a few well-loved verses, but they wouldn't fill the chasm of those kinds of questions. But over the years of walking with God, I have come to hold two things to be true that seem to contradict each other:

* God is sovereign, all-powerful.
* God is love, pure unadulterated love.

The tension lies in holding those with equal weight. If He is sovereign, then He could have stopped what happened. But He didn't, so how can He be love? And if His very essence is love and yet these terrible things happened, then surely He can't be all-powerful or He would have stopped them.

I believe God is both pure love *and* the one true almighty God. I have learned to bow my knees at this paradox.

God reminds us of how very different He is from you and me.

"My thoughts are nothing like your thoughts," says the LORD.
    "And my ways are far beyond anything you could imagine.
For just as the heavens are higher than the earth,
        so my ways are higher than your ways
        and my thoughts higher than your thoughts."
                    (Isa. 55:8–9)

Living a life of faith is so much more difficult than simply talking about it. God as a Father and yet an almighty, holy being is hard to grasp hold of. In my teens and twenties, I found it much easier to relate to the person of Jesus as a brother than to God as my Father. Jesus was kind and loving; He took up for the least likely one in a crowd and made everyone else leave him or her alone. I loved that. He loomed like the big brother who made sure the school bully knew, *If you want to get to her, you'll have to come through Me.* I loved God as my Father, but fear mixed with that love. I had blown it with one father; I couldn't afford to do that twice. The thoughts of regret and the longing for a do-over that ran through my mind as a young woman were unrealistic at best.

If only I could go back to that day when I was five and change the outcome.

If only I could have calmed my dad down so he would never have been taken away.

If I'd behaved better, he would never have become so angry.

If I hadn't tried to save myself, I wouldn't have lost my beloved protector.

I carried inside me this enormous weight of a failed mission, one for which I would never get a second chance. Or so I thought.

I dated the red-sports-car guy for a few weeks. He was funny, and he took me out to eat in restaurants I could never have afforded on my

Youth for Christ salary. I think part of the reason I wanted to be with him was that he was almost fourteen years older than I was, and I longed for a father's protection.

My two closest friends were against us dating. I couldn't understand why, as he treated me so well. But one night, Nancy and Raymond asked if I could take a little time with them. I agreed.

"We're concerned about this relationship," Nancy told me when we met up. She tucked a strand of blond hair behind her ears.

"What are you talking about?" I told myself not to be defensive, not to push back, because I knew a good Christian girl knew how to swallow feedback. Still, her words stung. They felt like an accusation.

"He's so much older than you," Raymond said.

"How can that matter?" I asked.

Nancy put her hand on mine. I saw tears in her eyes. "I don't know how to tell you this easily," she said, "so I'll just come out and say it. He's been divorced. And that's not all, he doesn't have a very good reputation, Sheila."

This alarmed me, and I assured them I'd talk to him about it.

As soon as I got an opportunity, I talked to him about my friends' concern.

"I made some poor choices in the past," he said. "But I'm a different person now."

I was grateful for his honesty. I was sure once my friends got to know him, they would change their minds. Weeks turned into months.

One evening he took me to a lovely little restaurant in Wales. Suddenly, he pulled out a box with a ring inside and knelt beside my chair. "Sheila, will you marry me?"

Overwhelmed, I said yes!

That night I would see my friends because we were leading a

conference together in Wales. I couldn't wait to tell them the news of my engagement.

I'll never forget Nancy's face. When I showed her the ring, tears ran down her cheeks. "Please," she said, "do not marry him."

Her words devastated me. I had hoped my friends would be happy for me, but they clearly were not.

But theirs weren't the only voices of dissent. The head of British Youth for Christ came to my house one evening. He told me, "Sheila, I hope you know how much I love you, how much my wife cares about you, how dear you are to our staff. We all love you."

I swallowed, trying to prepare myself for his *but*.

"But," he said, "we are all praying that you will reconsider this marriage."

No one in my life rejoiced with me.

As I think back on all of that now, I wonder why I closed myself off to their concern. To their very consistent words of caution. A healthy person would at least push things back a bit, take more time to be absolutely sure. The relentless onslaught had the opposite effect on me. I thought, *You just don't understand him. Yes, he's made some bad choices but he's different now.*

I honestly believe that if there had been no opposition, we would never have gotten married. I liked him a lot, but it was no great romance. In my heart, I determined that I would stand up for him no matter what. This time I would not abandon the one who had stepped heroically into the role of my protector.

Our wedding day was a sad affair. Not one of my friends attended. They told me that they would be there for me afterward, but they could not be part of the wedding. So only close family came. We had a fairly short service, then a nice meal in a local hotel before we got onto the A74 to head south. Sitting on the wet grass on the side of the road that night, blood dripping from my head onto my shoulder and looking at the accident scene of mangled cars and damaged lives, I thought out loud, "You fought everyone to be able to marry this man, and now it's done and no one cares anymore."

A girl will do almost anything to feel protected.

———&———

Sometimes others can't protect us, so we build walls around ourselves. These walls keep people out. They protect us. But they also cause us deep loneliness because we never allow people, no matter how many are in our lives, to know us. Being lonely has nothing to do with the number of people in your life. You can be lonely in a crowd, in church, or in a family gathering. I hear this phrase a lot from other women: "I feel so alone." I hear it from single women and married women, young and old, from lives that appear on the surface to be working well and those who are clearly in crisis. When you choose to live a vulnerable, transparent life as I have learned to do, you invite that in others too. It's a sacred trust that I never take lightly.

Recently, at the end of a conference in a small church in the Midwest, a woman (who told me up front that she was eighty-two) whispered to me, "I was raped when I was fourteen. I've never told another soul. I've lived a lonely life since then. I wanted to tell my father, but I was afraid he would stop loving me." She shed no tears for herself that night, but I did. I thought of all the relationships she must have had in her life—parents, siblings, friends who never got to see over the wall she'd erected around her heart to keep her safe—and that had effectively kept her alone.

The reason I have always been drawn to the story of King David is that, although he seriously messed up many times, he had such an out-loud, honest, vibrant relationship with God. Even when David tended sheep by himself, he was clearly never alone, and he knew who his protector was. He wasn't careful in his ongoing dialogue with God. If you read some of the psalms, they would never have made it into our twenty-first-century church libraries. Think about these examples:

I am silent before you; I won't say a word,
  for my punishment is from you.
But please stop striking me!
  I am exhausted by the blows from your hand.
When you discipline us for our sins,
  you consume like a moth what is precious to us.
  Each of us is but a breath. . . .

Hear my prayer, O Lord!
  Listen to my cries for help!
  Don't ignore my tears.
For I am your guest—
  a traveler passing through,
  as my ancestors were before me.
Leave me alone so I can smile again
  before I am gone and exist no more.
                    (Ps. 39:9–13)

O Lord, how long will you forget me? Forever?
  How long will you look the other way?
How long must I struggle with anguish in my soul,
  with sorrow in my heart every day?
  How long will my enemy have the upper hand?
Turn and answer me, O Lord my God!
                    (Ps.13:1–3)

Can you imagine praying gut-honest like that?

Please stop striking me!
Leave me alone so I can smile again!
Hey! You, God, turn and answer me!

Yet, this is the one who was twice called a man after God's own heart. There's something to his honesty that we need to press in and dig deep to find. I'm hungry to be that kind of real woman.

I've spent the past few months studying 1 and 2 Samuel. I have made a habit of reading all David's psalms out loud. One thing has become crystal clear to me. David may have hidden from King Saul at times, he may have pretended to lose his mind to save his life (see 1 Sam. 21:12–13), but he never hid from God or forsook His protection. David knew in the depths of his being that the only one he could run to for protection was the Lord. In the solitude of his early years as a shepherd boy, he had learned this important truth.

Out in the cold nights watching the sheep, or moving them on to fresh pasture over the fields where Ruth had gleaned fallen grain, David stayed in constant communication with the Lord. His love for God poured out of his heart:

> *The LORD is my shepherd;*
> *I have all that I need. . . .*
> *Even when I walk*
> *through the darkest valley,*
> *I will not be afraid,*
> *for you are close beside me.*
> *Your rod and your staff*
> *protect and comfort me.*
> (Ps. 23:1–4)

David was utterly convinced that the unseen One was the only one worth pursuing, the only one whose protection mattered. Because he knew of God's constant care and presence, he could (and would) face giants. Long before he confronted Goliath, he had already become a giant slayer.

When a young David told King Saul that he would fight Goliath,

Saul didn't take him seriously. After all, he was a teenage shepherd boy. Listen to David's response:

> I have been taking care of my father's sheep and goats . . . When a lion or a bear comes to steal a lamb from the flock, I go after it with a club and rescue the lamb from its mouth. If the animal turns on me, I catch it by the jaw and club it to death. I have done this to both lions and bears, and I'll do it to this pagan Philistine, too, for he has defied the armies of the living God! The LORD who rescued me from the claws of the lion and the bear will rescue me from this Philistine! (1 Sam. 17:34–37)

There's a lot we can glean from this chapter of David's life. He faithfully pursued God when no one watched. He showed up with courage and confidence to defend the helpless, even when they were only sheep. Every strength he possessed as the king of Israel developed in the place where no one applauded or noticed him. No one but God. We may long for a father's protection, but young David learned that when everyone else failed him, even his father, God would always protect him. In the same way, when our longing is directed toward God, we'll never be left empty and alone. That conviction took David from the sheepfold to a battlefield no other man was brave enough to engage.

Before you are tempted to say, "Well, David was a mighty man who would go on to prove himself to be a great leader. How can I relate to that?" let me remind you of this scene from his early life. When Samuel the prophet examined the cream of the crop of Jesse's sons, David's father didn't even summon him. Samuel, then, instinctively thought that Eliab, the strong and tall eldest son, would be God's choice for a king. But God said to him, "Don't judge by his appearance or height, for I have rejected him. The LORD doesn't see things the way you see them. People judge by outward appearance, but the LORD looks at the heart" (1 Sam. 16:7).

This same Eliab cowered along with Saul's army when Goliath

threatened the nation. He was as terrified as every other man. David was the only one who understood a life-altering truth: No matter how big the giant you face right now, God is bigger. He is the protecting One.

Let's back up a little and set the scene. Israel's army was in a very vulnerable and dangerous situation. Enemies could approach the heartland of Judah from the coast through six valleys. The Philistines already controlled two of them: Socoh and Azekah. Now they streamed through the valley of Elah. If they gained more ground, they would threaten Bethlehem, Hebron, and Saul's capital city, Gibeah.

The valley of Elah was a huge canyon, almost a mile wide. On either side, the mountain sloped up for about half a mile. The Philistine army had gathered on one side of the canyon, with Israel's army facing them on the other. Every morning and evening for forty days, the Philistine champion, Goliath, the Rocky of his day, issued his defiant challenge: "'Why are you all coming out to fight? . . . I am the Philistine champion, but you are only the servants of Saul. Choose one man to come down here and fight me! If he kills me, then we will be your slaves. But if I kill him, you will be our slaves! I defy the armies of Israel today! Send me a man who will fight me!'" (1 Sam. 17:8–10).

What he suggested was hardly a fair fight. Let's take a look at what we know about Goliath. Traditionally we read that Goliath was "six cubits and a span" (v. 14 ESV). A cubit is about eighteen inches, and a span is about nine. So that would put Goliath at nine feet nine inches— serious NBA forward here! That's the Goliath we first encounter in Sunday school and Bible picture storybooks. We get that figure from what's called the Masoretic Text (MT), meaning the "received" Hebrew text on which most of the Old Testament is based. In the Septuagint manuscripts (the Greek LXX), however, Goliath is given a shorter height of six feet nine inches. For most of the modern era, though, the LXX has been viewed as a secondary source, not as accurate as the MT.

You may remember, however, that between 1947 and 1956,

documents called the Dead Sea Scrolls were discovered in eleven caves along the northwest shore of the Dead Sea. Several small fragments were from 1 and 2 Samuel. Some parts were badly damaged, but one large piece (4QSam), 1 Samuel 17:3–6, is very clear. This is by far the oldest Hebrew manuscript ever discovered, and in it, Goliath is six feet nine inches tall.

If you stayed with me through all of that, you may wonder why I included it. I mention it for one reason alone. Clearly it doesn't really matter how tall Goliath was. Either way he was a very big guy—and mean. But if indeed he was six foot nine, he would have been about the same height as King Saul, who was known to be a good head and shoulders above other men (see 1 Sam. 9:2). In other words that would have been much more of a fair fight—one tall champion against another. The truth revealed in this passage is that Saul may have had a champion's height, but he did not have a champion's heart. That rested in a shepherd boy alone.

We read that for forty days, morning and evening, Goliath strutted his stuff before the Israelites, repeating his taunting challenge. When I'm facing a Goliath in my life, some mountain that I can't even begin to imagine how to climb over, the doubts hit me hardest morning and evening. Don't you find that? You wake up in the morning and the first thing that hits you is the reality that the mountain is still there. When you finally fall in bed at night, worry creeps in with you, reminding you of the same insurmountable mountain. Scripture tells us that Goliath's daily threats worked, causing the Israelites to doubt God's protection: "When Saul and the Israelites heard this, they were terrified and deeply shaken" (1 Sam. 17:11).

David was too young to fight in the army, but one day his father, Jesse, asked him to take food to his brothers to discover how they were doing. So David asked another shepherd to keep an eye on his sheep while he ran this errand for his dad. It must have been quite a sight for a boy. He would have been about the age of a junior in high school as he left his house in Bethlehem and made his way up and over the Judean mountains to the army's camp.

As he crested the final rise, the army spread out like locusts across the hillside. Quite a sight if you're used to seeing flocks of sheep. The men cried out as if they were ready for battle. David was excited to see what was going to happen. "David left his things with the keeper of supplies and hurried out to the ranks to greet his brothers. As he was talking with them, Goliath, the Philistine champion from Gath, came out from the Philistine ranks. Then David heard him shout his usual taunt to the army of Israel" (1 Sam. 17:22–23).

We read that the soldiers were terrified and headed back to their tents, leaving this boy standing there listening to Goliath's challenge. Enraged, David couldn't believe that Goliath would dare to insult the army of his God. This was the forty-first day the Israelites heard this mocking challenge, yet once more they ran and hid. But this was the first time David had heard Goliath's taunts. David stood his ground. I love how he perceived Goliath. "Who is this pagan Philistine anyway, that he is allowed to defy the armies of the living God?" (v. 26).

King Saul had tried to sweeten the pot for his soldiers by offering one of his daughters in marriage, great wealth, and no taxes for life to the one who would kill Goliath. The sad thing? Saul was the only one qualified for the job, taller than any of them. He was their leader. But Saul wasn't walking closely with God, and when you're not walking closely with God, giants loom enormous while God's promised protection sinks. David's protector was God—so that kind of faith reduced Goliath to size.

It's worth noting that on every one of the previous forty days, "Goliath stood and shouted a taunt across to the Israelites. 'Why are you all coming out to fight?'" (1 Sam. 17:8). On the forty-first day, however, we read, "And the men of Israel said, 'Have you seen this man *who has come up?* Surely he has come up to defy Israel'" (v. 25 ESV, emphasis added). Goliath was now on the move. He neared the Israelite army. Fear is like that. If you don't challenge it in the name of the Lord, fear will occupy more and more territory of your heart and mind. Everything good and righteous inside of David rose up as he asked, "Who is this uncircumcised Philistine?"

You might be tempted to think that David's brothers would have been proud of their little brother. Unfortunately that was not the case. When a family operates on one set of unwritten rules, then when one member breaks the pattern, deciding not to live in fear anymore, he ends up rocking the boat for everyone else. People like their comfort, the way things have always been. They don't take kindly to upstarts. And to his brothers, David was an upstart: "But when David's oldest brother, Eliab, heard David talking to the men, he was angry. 'What are you doing around here anyway?' he demanded. 'What about those few sheep you're supposed to be taking care of? I know about your pride and deceit. You just want to see the battle!'" (1 Sam. 17:28).

Can you hear the put-down in his tone, even using the phrase "few sheep"? Eliab remembered the day when he had been presented to Samuel, yet passed over for his puny younger brother. He remembered Samuel pouring anointing oil over David's head, when surely he should have been the chosen one. The takeaway? Don't be surprised if you're attacked when you determine, by God's grace, not to live in fear anymore but instead confront every Goliath in your life, bravely believing God to be your protector. Fear didn't stop David, and we mustn't let it stop us.

When Saul heard that someone asked to face Goliath, he wanted to see him. I'm sure he expected it would be someone who looked burly and muscular. So when he saw David, he was disgusted and told him not to be ridiculous. "Saul finally consented. 'All right, go ahead,' he said. 'And may the LORD be with you!' " (1 Sam. 17:37).

That last sentence makes me smile. It has that "bless your heart" tone to it! I'm sure Saul thought that David had about ten minutes left to live. To give him even the semblance of a fighting chance, he offered David his armor—fit for a tall, fighting king. David couldn't even walk in it. Another lesson: Never try on someone else's armor. It won't fit. Don't try to be the next Beth Moore or Christine Caine; God already has them. We need you!

So David took the armor off, picked up five smooth stones from the river, and put them in his shepherd's bag. With sling in hand, he set out to face Goliath.

Can you picture that? Not only was Goliath an extremely tall man, by any manuscript's assessment, but he was also well dressed for battle. "He wore a bronze helmet, and his bronze coat of mail weighed 125 pounds. He also wore bronze leg armor, and he carried a bronze javelin on his shoulder. The shaft of his spear was as heavy and thick as a weaver's beam, tipped with an iron spearhead that weighed 15 pounds. His armor bearer walked ahead of him carrying a shield" (1 Sam. 17:5–7).

When Goliath saw David approach him, he was furious. It looked as though the Israelites were trying to make a fool of him, sending out their mascot:

> Goliath walked out toward David with his shield bearer ahead of him, sneering in contempt at this ruddy-faced boy. "Am I a dog," he roared at David, "that you come at me with a stick?" And he cursed David by the names of his gods. "Come over here, and I'll give your flesh to the birds and wild animals!" Goliath yelled. (vv. 41–44)

It's interesting how the enemy's guard is down when we don't look much like soldiers. But let me tell you, girls, God is raising up for Himself a ragtag band of women who are tired of listening to the bellyaching of the Goliaths in our lives, and we are ready to come against them in the name of the Lord! Why? Because we know God is our protector.

David ignored the insults Goliath threw at him and replied, "You come to me with sword, spear, and javelin, but I come to you in the name of the LORD of Heaven's Armies—the God of the armies of Israel, whom you have defied. Today the LORD will conquer you, and I will kill you and cut off your head" (1 Sam. 17:45–46).

I love that! David made it clear he had no thought of conquering Goliath. That was God's job. He just got to kill him and chop off his head. This is a key principle for all potential giant slayers—the battle is the Lord's! "Not by might, nor by power, but by my Spirit, says the LORD of hosts" (Zech. 4:6 ESV).

So David put one stone into his sling, and he raised it above his head. For a moment the air was filled with the swishing of leather as it gained speed. Then David released the stone. It flew directly to its target, right in the center of Goliath's forehead. The giant fell facedown, dead, before the shepherd boy.

With their bully gone, the Philistines retreated with the Israelites in hot pursuit. A lot of blood spilled that day, but none of it was Israelite blood. David made his way to Saul's tent, still holding the severed head of Goliath.

" 'Tell me about your father, young man,' Saul said" (1 Sam. 17:58).

A lot of life-altering stories start with that one question. Including mine. Including yours.

And the truth is, our Father in heaven is in the business of protecting us.

For some of us it takes a long time to believe that. For Pam (not her real name), it saved her life.

I met her on a prison visit. The warden had given me permission after speaking to the general prison population to spend time with any women who wanted to speak privately. Several younger women shared horrific stories of abuse and violence. For many of them prison had become the first place they felt protected. Pam was the last in line. She looked to be in her forties, with tattoos on her arms and neck and a scar over her left eye.

Pam said something to me that night I'll never forget: "God brought me to prison to set me free." When I asked her what she meant, she told me about a life of violence. Her dad was a drunk and at his worst would beat her mother, and when Pam attempted to intervene, beat her too. She grew up tormented by fear. "So I joined a gang," she said. "I determined that nobody would ever hit me again. I'd learn how to protect myself." This was her fifth time in prison. Her latest conviction carried a long sentence.

She told me that one night in her cell she cried out to God: "If You're real, then I need You to show me right now."

There was no bolt of lightning or thunderous voice, but God showed up that night for Pam. She described what happened to her.

"It was like I was standing under a waterfall and everything dirty was being washed away and I was clean . . . really clean, for the first time."

We talked until the guard said it was time for her to go back to her cell. I asked Pam one final question. "Are you still afraid?"

She smiled as she got up to leave. "No, not anymore. God's got my back now."

Pam's story is extreme. Most of us will never find ourselves in prison, but I wonder if you ever feel imprisoned by fear. The truth that was restoring Pam's soul is a truth for you and me. God is our protector. He is our hiding place. He is with those who turn to Him in prison and those who turn to Him in pews and parking spots and private bedrooms across the earth. David proclaimed that truth as a boy on the hillside, and it carried him to face a giant in the valley. He sang out what he knew was true so it would be louder than any fear that tried to sneak in the back door of his heart. It's not a bad idea!

A few months ago I put together a worship playlist of those songs that remind me when I feel small and vulnerable that God is on the throne and He is mighty to save. I highly recommend that you do the same.

THREE

The Longing for What Used to Be

I didn't know then what I wanted, but
the ache for it was palpable.[1]
—*Sue Monk Kidd*

As soon as the boy was gone, David came
out from where he had been hiding near the
stone pile. Then David bowed three times to
Jonathan with his face to the ground. Both
of them were in tears as they embraced each
other and said good-bye, especially David.
—*1 Samuel 20:41*

MY HUSBAND, BARRY, IS PASSIONATE ABOUT
magnolia trees. Actually, he's more passionate about ripping the branches
from magnolia trees and decorating every square inch of our home
with the deep green, almost waxy leaves that continue to flourish even
when the flowers have faded and fallen. Because he was raised in South
Carolina, magnolias say home to him, particularly at Christmastime.
I associate the season with tinsel, chocolate Santas, and large, colored
bulbs on our Scottish Christmas tree, but for Barry it's magnolia gar-
lands on everything that doesn't move.

When we were first married in December 1994, we lived in a small apartment in Nashville, Tennessee. The apartment was lovely but bereft of a single magnolia tree in the surrounding area. I wondered how Barry would survive. In retrospect I should have anticipated the crime spree that loomed!

One evening, just a few days before Christmas, he suggested we go for a drive. It wasn't a nice night; it was cold and raining hard.

"Let's just light a fire and stay home," I suggested. "No one's out in this weather tonight."

"I know," he said. "It's perfect!"

We drove down Twenty-First Street as sleet battered the windshield. He slowed down as we approached a large, beautiful, and well-known church in Nashville, set on lavish grounds.

"Okay," he said, with the nervous intensity of a novice crook, "when I pull to the curb, run out and grab as many branches as you can from that large magnolia tree!"

"Are you kidding me?" I yelled. "I'm not grabbing anything from anywhere!"

"You have to. It's a Christmas emergency! Go!"

I still can't account for this departure from a previously intact moral code, but I leapt like a lemming from the passenger side of the car and began to randomly grab a few soaking-wet branches. Clutching the stolen goods, I ran back to the car, scrambled in, and yelled, "Hit it!"

That Christmas crime lurked in the basement of my soul as I waited to be arrested at any moment. The only way to quiet my screaming conscience was that the next time I visited that denuded campus, I left an inordinate amount in the offering plate!

It's funny the things that remind us of other times and other places. It might be a fragrance or a song, but whatever it is, we find ourselves pulled back through the years, longing for a time that used to be, a time when life seemed simpler. In short, we are nostalgic beings at our core.

I see that wistfulness in my mother now. The early stages of Alzheimer's are robbing her of recent years and memories, placing them on a shelf too high to reach. What is present and real for her is what used to be. The last time I was home in Scotland, we went for a walk in the park across the street from her white stone cottage. We took it slowly, stopping to rest on a bench and watch children play on the swing set.

When she was ready to head back home, she turned left out of the park's gate, the opposite direction from her little house.

"It's this way, Mum," I said, pointing to the right.

She paused for a moment, confused. Then I realized she was headed for the house she had lived in when she was a child—same street, different direction. She followed me, but I could tell that her heart went the other way.

There are many telltale signs that what is true at the moment continues to be swallowed up by what used to be for Mum. She doesn't seem surprised that I'm fifty-nine but has forgotten that she is eighty-four. Some days she is shocked when she looks in the mirror and sees an old woman. In her mind she is in her twenties, with all of life ahead of her.

It's a hard thing to watch your parents get old and every day lose little pieces of who they are. Yet I understand that's simply the legacy of our lives on a broken planet.

The longing, it continues.

Perhaps for you the longing for what used to be has nothing to do with the ravages of age but with the place you stand right now.

You find yourself in a loveless marriage. You never saw that coming.

The child who was such a joy is now almost unrecognizable to you, rebellious and distant.

You may have lost the one you love and you long for what used to be when you remember being happy.

Perhaps you've overcommitted yourself financially and you ache to go back to when life was simpler and you didn't have to work so hard just to make ends meet. You dread the day you can't.

That kind of longing is a very tough place to live. Regret is a relentless taskmaster, a place devoid of hope because there's nothing we can do about our current lot; we can't turn the clock back. We can't jump into a time machine and dial in the days that used to be.

I wonder if that's what was on the heart and mind of King Solomon when he wrote, "Don't long for 'the good old days.' This is not wise" (Eccl. 7:10). Yet for some, this longing seems inescapable.

I once had a conversation with a woman I met in an airport. She recognized me from an event at which I'd spoken at her church and asked if I had a few minutes to chat. My flight didn't leave for an hour, so I suggested we grab a cup of coffee. We sat down opposite each other at a quiet table in the corner of the terminal coffee shop. I didn't have to ask a single question; I just listened as her story literally poured out of her as if it had been dammed up for months.

She had met her husband when they were both students. She had studied nursing and he had pursued a career as a surgeon. His was a much longer degree program, so as soon as she graduated, she began working immediately to support them both. The pace was hard, but she took extra shifts and accepted the fact that their first few years of marriage weren't going to be much of a honeymoon.

"I was proud of him though," she said. "He's very smart, and he works so hard. I didn't mind making the sacrifices I had to make."

She paused for a moment. As she spoke again, her voice caught in her throat, letting out a noise almost like a small animal caught in a trap. Her shoulders shook as tears coursed down her cheeks.

I put my hand over hers. "Just take your time," I said.

"Well, he finally finished! It was such a long road. Four years of undergraduate school, four years of medical school, and then three years of surgical residency. But we did it!"

She dug in her purse for a tissue. When she looked up again, her eyes had changed. A storm raged there.

"In his fourth year as a surgical resident, he left me for a surgical nurse!" she said. "Can you believe that?" she said, louder than I think she realized. "I sweat blood and tears to put him through school. I put all my dreams of starting a family in my twenties on hold for him, and that's what I get! What am I supposed to do now?"

I got her a glass of water and sat beside her, noting her age, trying to make sense of her story. "I am so desperately sorry," I began. "I can't imagine what that must feel like. When did he leave?"

"Twenty-one years ago," she said.

I sat there, stunned by her answer.

Twenty-one years, stuck in what used to be and never will be again.

Twenty-one years of longing for the days when they were young and in love and working toward one common goal.

Twenty-one years looking in the rearview mirror of her life.

Twenty-one years of lying in bed at night, replaying the events, the sacrifices, the tears, and the bitter words that brought her dream to a shattering conclusion.

I asked if I could pray for her. She nodded her head and laid it down on her hands on the green Formica tabletop.

"Father God," I began, "thank You that You see us here in this little coffee shop. I lift my broken and battered sister to You now. You know her whole story, and You love her passionately. Lord, You have caught every tear, heard every cry, and understood every moment of anger that has shaken her fragile frame. She needs new hope, Lord. She needs peace. She needs to know that You still have a plan for her life, that she is not simply a victim of someone else's choices. Will You speak life back into a heart on hold? In Jesus' name, amen."

I had ten minutes to board my flight, so I hugged her and told her I would keep praying for her. I have. I only hope she has moved on.

Even though her story is an extreme case of longing paralyzing your life, I relate to some of her feelings. Can you? Days when life seemed simpler . . .

After I graduated from seminary and before my first husband and I married, I worked for Youth for Christ. I loved it. We had to raise our own support, which was challenging but also encouraging. It was humbling to see people from my home church get behind the ministry into which God had called me. Some weeks I spoke with my team of school evangelists, and other weeks I traveled with Clive Calver, head of British Youth for Christ, and my boss, Graham Kendrick. Clive would speak, and Graham and I would lead worship. I loved being part of a team. I loved belonging.

We didn't stay in hotels in those days. Members of whatever church we worked with that week offered us accommodations. I met some lovely people and some really interesting people, like the lady who insisted that I share a bedroom with her twelve—yes, I said *twelve*—cats! Or the family that, once we were ready to call it a night, backed their car out of the garage, put up a camping bed, and wished me a good night. It was so cold I had to put on everything I had in my suitcase to survive till morning. Someday I might write a book *Tales from the Road*, but for now let's just say it was an adventure. Even so, I was doing what I loved to do. I got to tell people about the love of Jesus. I didn't have much money, but I was happy.

After John and I married, I longed for those simple days. Because I had refused to listen to the counsel of my leadership, I was asked to leave Youth for Christ. John and I moved into his lovely little house in north London. Very involved in the Christian music world, he ran his own record label and was determined that I was to become the next "big thing" in contemporary Christian music. I didn't want to be a "big thing." I only wanted to serve God. I knew instinctively that I was too broken to bear the scrutiny and pressure of a world where you are continually judged on your last performance.

The next few years are honestly a blur to me.

I remember photo shoots and celebrity diets, because you can't be a star if you're twenty pounds over skinny.

I remember relocating to America because that's where all the big tours were.

I remember touring the United States with Phil Keaggy and Russ Taff, night after night after night of concerts and motels.

I remember the Christian Artist Seminar held at Estes Park in Colorado. Each artist (and *everyone* was there) had twenty minutes to blow everyone away. If you didn't get a standing ovation, you failed. An artist friend of mine told me that John had slipped someone money to make sure that the sound and lights were better for me than for the artist who performed before me. I didn't believe that could be true. After the event that night, all the artists were invited to a little cabin for supper. I found a quiet moment and told John what my friend had said. He looked at me as if I had crawled off Noah's ark and told me that everybody did it. That made me feel sick to my stomach. I was becoming well known but I didn't like my life. I was very lonely.

Suddenly, I could relate to Job when he said, "Lying in bed, I think, 'When will it be morning?' But the night drags on, and I toss till dawn" (Job 7:4).

As I look back on those days from the place I stand now, I clearly see the mercy of God at every turn. There is nothing like the heat of a spotlight to reveal what is in us. The fire of a crucible brings the dirt and dross to the surface. It's mercy, a severe mercy but mercy nonetheless. I became acutely aware of my insecurity, fear, and shame. I had such a deep longing for a father figure to take care of me. Not only that, but I believed that although I had been unable to save my dad, perhaps I could save John. As the crowd of those who judged him for the life he had lived in the past grew stronger, my will to stand beside him and show them they were wrong intensified. I knew who he could be. And he knew who I could be—a Christian superstar. But neither of us wanted the other's vision.

During that time I felt as if I were falling down a well while my voice grew fainter every day. I had no idea then that when you fall down, down, down for a long time and finally lie bloodied, bruised, and broken on the rocky bottom, you can actually find what you've really been longing for the whole time. Yes, mine was a long, dark fall, seemingly endless and fatal. But when I hit bottom, Jesus was there. I'll write more about that later, but for now know this: the choices you make in the darkness when no one but God is watching will impact the rest of your life.

Just ask David and King Saul.

―――∞――

When we left David, the scent of victory permeated him. A young shepherd boy had accomplished what no warrior would even attempt; he'd felled a giant. Life changed for David that day. He wasn't allowed to return to the life he knew. "From that day on Saul kept David with him and wouldn't let him return home," we are told. "Whatever Saul asked David to do, David did it successfully. So Saul made him a commander over the men of war, an appointment that was welcomed by the people and Saul's officers alike" (1 Sam. 18:2, 5).

Quite a leap from shepherd boy to commander of the army, but perhaps not quite the leap it might seem to us. Consider the hours David had spent alone with the sheep out under the stars, keeping watch over every one. He'd practiced his skill with a sling over and over until, with one stone, he could sever a branch from a tree far in the distance. One day a bear had lurked near one of his beloved little lambs, so armed with no fear but with pinpoint accuracy, he'd killed it. I imagine him picking up that little one and saying, "Just as I am your shepherd, the Lord of Hosts is mine."

Goliath? Just the next bear in line.

In the solitude of his life, David became one of the greatest hymn writers this world has ever known. It's believed that the first psalm David wrote was the Twenty-third Psalm. He penned it after Samuel had anointed him, yet while he was still shepherding his sheep. The young David sang out in the fields, to the sheep, to the stars, to the angels, and to his Father's heart:

> The LORD is my shepherd;
>   I have all that I need.
> He lets me rest in green meadows;
>   he leads me beside peaceful streams.
>   He renews my strength.
> He guides me along right paths,
>   bringing honor to his name.
> Even when I walk
>   through the darkest valley,
> I will not be afraid,
>   for you are close beside me.
> Your rod and your staff
>   protect and comfort me.
> You prepare a feast for me
>   in the presence of my enemies.

You honor me by anointing my head with oil.
   My cup overflows with blessings.
Surely your goodness and unfailing love will pursue me
   all the days of my life,
and I will live in the house of the LORD
   forever.

(Ps. 23)

He sang words then that he would need in the lonely and danger-ous months and years ahead, because when King Saul saw the way the people loved David, he did what all people who have not surrendered to the sovereignty of God do when they feel their position is threatened: he plotted to take him out. David didn't see Saul's rage coming because he'd done nothing to deserve it. In fact Saul's evil plans came on the heels of David's victory over Goliath.

When the victorious Israelite army was returning home after David had killed the Philistine, women from all the towns of Israel came out to meet King Saul. They sang and danced for joy with tambourines and cymbals. This was their song:

> *"Saul has killed his thousands,*
>   *and David his ten thousands!"*

This made Saul very angry. "What's this?" he said. "They credit David with ten thousands and me with only thousands. Next they'll be making him their king!" So from that time on Saul kept a jealous eye on David. (1 Sam. 18:6–8)

✳ Jealousy and insecurity are soul cancers. If they are not dealt with swiftly and mercilessly, they spread, destroying everything they touch.

44

King Saul didn't start out like this. Do you remember his beginnings? He was Israel's first king, chosen by God. He came from a strong, godly line; Abraham, Isaac, and Moses were his ancestors. Under his leadership, the nation of Israel was unified. He formed a great army and won important battles under the power of God. Saul was also a prophet. When the Spirit of God fell upon him, he prophesied with great power and authority. In addition, Saul was tall and handsome, and he had great charisma.

In fact, Saul had all the outward appearance of a great man of God, the kind we would put on a platform and line up to listen to. But Scripture reminds us that God alone sees what's in a person's heart, no matter how amazing he appears. While we might be wooed by charisma, God examines the character. Before David ever appeared on the scene, cracks had appeared in Saul's soul armor.

Three times he had disobeyed a command of God. (See 1 Sam. 13:8–15; 14:24–45; 15:10–21 for further study.) When the prophet Samuel challenged him, Saul tried to justify his choices. He didn't realize that privilege brings responsibility, but it doesn't suppose entitlement. Whenever we think that our position in leadership supersedes the Word of God we are in deep trouble. Disobedience to God's ways becomes a slippery slope. The first wayward step is usually hard, but the next one is easier. And before long, you become unrecognizable as the person you once were—from a person of greatness who elevated the greatness of God, to a self-absorbed "god" yourself. Before David the young shepherd boy ever came face-to-face with Saul, we read these tragic words, "And the LORD was sorry he had ever made Saul king of Israel" (1 Sam. 15:35).

So what were Saul's choices? God chose another to be king over Israel. The people didn't know that yet, but Saul and the prophet Samuel did. Having grieved God to such an extent, what roads were left open to him now?

I imagine bumping into him in an airport coffee shop. At a green,

Formica-topped table, he tells me that God has moved on and chosen someone else to be king, so what's he supposed to do now?

That's the question we all have to answer: What do you do when you long for what used to be or what you used to have, and you can't have it anymore? Perhaps in your own life you used to hold a position that you no longer hold, and you long for all it represented, but it was given to someone else. So now you sit rehashing the good old days, living with regret today, idolizing the nostalgia of the past.

It might have been a friendship that went sour. Too many harsh words spoken between you, so your former friend has moved on. What do you do when you bump into her with her new best friend?

Perhaps you were married and are now widowed and you long for the days when you shared every moment with your husband; now the house is strangely quiet.

You may have a child who has wandered away from faith and from family, and the longing for what used to be is heartbreaking.

I don't know what you are facing, but I do know that what you choose to believe when things go sour will impact the rest of your life.

What were King Saul's options? I see only two.

1. He could fall on his face before God and ask Him for forgiveness. In humility he could relinquish the crown to save his own soul, his own life.
2. He could determine that no one, not even God, would rob him of who he used to be. He could hunt down the Lord's anointed (David) and drive him out into the night and usher in years of misery. If he chose this path he would fall, but not on his face before God. Ultimately, he would fall on his own sword.

As you know from Scripture, Saul chose option 2. It would cost him his life, but not before he made David's life unbearable.

If Saul's antagonism to David was extreme, so, too, was his son Jonathan's love for and devotion to David. Many writers paint pictures of David and Jonathan as if they were two giddy teenagers, but that's far from the truth. You had to be twenty to be in the Israelite army (Num. 1:3). David was only eighteen, but Saul had made him a high-ranking officer in the hopes he would be killed in battle. Jonathan was already commanding a third of the army and had won two great victories. Warren Wiersbe, in his Old Testament Bible commentary, suggests an age closer to forty for Jonathan.[2] It is significant that Jonathan stood next in line to the throne. Although he was a mature, seasoned officer, he recognized the hand of God on his friend David and, unlike his father, submitted to God's choice. Clearly Jonathan longed more for the will of God than for his own position.

Let's sit for a moment with David and try to imagine how drastically his life had changed since the days he sat out under the stars, watching his sheep and singing his heart out to God. He had taken out the monster Goliath. This victory had ushered him into the royal court. Not only that, but King Saul had betrothed his daughter Michal to David as his bride. This made Saul David's father-in-law. These should have been the best days of his life. David was with a woman who loved him. God was with him, and he experienced tremendous victory in the battles he led.

But Saul was in a really-bad-becoming-mad place. Think about it. What king sits at home with a spear in his hand (in the safest house in the land), on edge, ready to strike at whatever he perceives threatens him? When you reject God and the joy of His covering over your life, you leave yourself open to all sorts of evil and paranoid thoughts. It's interesting, though, to read in 1 Samuel 19:9–10 that the disturbing spirit that came on Saul was from God. "But one day when Saul was sitting at home, with spear in hand, the tormenting spirit from the LORD suddenly came upon him again. As David played his harp, Saul hurled his spear at David. But David dodged out of the way, and leaving the spear stuck in the wall, he fled and escaped into the night."

Was this tormenting spirit an indication of the mercy of God? Was God giving Saul a chance to own how terrible his life had become and repent—body, soul, and spirit? We don't know, but what we do know is that rather than resisting the evil that slowly overtook him, Saul welcomed it, gave it free rein.

None of this madness made sense to David. He'd done nothing wrong. He simply wanted to serve the king, play his harp to soothe Saul during his troubled bouts, fight when he was called on to lead, and love his wife. Those are honest, noble dreams. But one slowly disintegrating king stood in the way. Though David knew he would be king, he resisted what must've been a longing in him and instead gave in to patience as he watched God's sovereign plan unfold before him.

Have you ever been in a place where one person is actively ruining everything for you? It might be her jealousy or a personality conflict or that she observes you wanting to live your life honoring God and it really bugs her.

What speaks volumes about the kind of heart David had was how he handled that spear. Most men, had a spear been thrown at *them* and it lodged in the wall (and not for the first time), would pull that thing out and throw it right back. Not David. Even though he had already been anointed as king, he refused to grab the throne for himself. He left the timing of his rise or his fall to God. So he ran. Fleeing was not a cowardly move. It takes courage to run from those in power who have lost the ability to hear God's voice.

First Samuel 20 describes the heartbreaking conversation when David sought out Jonathan to see if his friend could help him understand why Saul pursued him. It's clear that Jonathan didn't really understand the extent of his father's mad hatred.

> "What have I done?" he exclaimed. "What is my crime? How have I offended your father that he is so determined to kill me?"
>
> "That's not true!" Jonathan protested. "You're not going to die. He always tells me everything he's going to do, even the little things. I know my father wouldn't hide something like this from me. It just isn't so!"
>
> Then David took an oath before Jonathan and said, "Your father knows perfectly well about our friendship, so he has said to himself, 'I won't tell Jonathan—why should I hurt him?' But I swear to you that I am only a step away from death! I swear it by the LORD and by your own soul!"
>
> "Tell me what I can do to help you," Jonathan exclaimed. (1 Sam. 20:1–4)

So they came up with a plan. Instead of taking his place at the king's table for the monthly feast, David would stay away. If Saul asked where he was, Jonathan would explain that he had gone to the yearly sacrifice at Bethlehem with his family, which would be reasonable and should be understood. If Saul didn't object, it would indicate that David was safe; but if the king became furious because David had once again slipped out of his hands, then Jonathan would finally understand that David's life was at stake.

It went as David expected. Saul was so furious that he threw his spear at Jonathan, his own son. Jonathan was angry with his father and heartbroken for his friend.

Jonathan and David had agreed that the next day David would hide in a prearranged place, and Jonathan would give him a sign indicating whether or not David could safely come home to the palace. "I will come out and shoot three arrows . . . as though I were shooting at a target.

Then I will send a boy to bring the arrows back." The agreement was that if it weren't safe for David to return, Jonathan would shoot the arrows far beyond his young servant. When the boy went to fetch them, Jonathan would tell him, "Go farther—the arrows are still ahead of you" (v. 22). We know what happened.

Once the servant boy had retrieved the arrows, Jonathan sent him back to town, and David came out of hiding. The story concludes, "Then David bowed three times to Jonathan with his face to the ground. Both of them were in tears as they embraced each other and said good-bye, especially David" (v. 41).

No going back. Saul's wrathful choices had been made. Doors slammed closed.

David would enter the crucible of suffering where truly great servants of God are made.

Perhaps you are there now. One of the most devastating realities of this kind of suffering is that often the one you thought would be your protector becomes the one who measures out the pain. All that longing for justice, for fairness, for having everything as it should be seems useless. As you think on the glory days of the past, your heart aches to turn back the clock, but you can't. In these moments it's tempting to believe that God has forgotten about us, or even worse, that He simply doesn't care—His favor has moved on. If you are there right now, my heart aches for you. No one signs up for this school of suffering, and yet the deep work that God does in this painful, lonely place is rarely produced anywhere else.

So have you been abandoned? Never! You just have to remember in those moments of betrayal that God is still in control no matter how things appear. In the meantime you may need to find a safe place to hide.

When you search for a haven to hide in, make it under the shadow of His wings. David could have longed to go back to that simple life under the stars, with sheep as his companions and all of heaven as the audience to his songs of praise, but he couldn't go back and neither can you. Once you've killed a Goliath, life changes and God calls you forward, always forward. If you remain focused on longing for what was, you'll miss what is and what is to come.

The horizon may be dim and overcast at the moment, but trust God. He is for you, and new things are on the way.

FOUR

The Longing for Control

Be not angry that you cannot make others
as you wish them to be, since you cannot
make yourself as you wish to be.[1]
—*Thomas à Kempis, The Imitation of Christ*

Better to be patient than powerful;
  better to have self-control than to conquer a city.
  —*Proverbs 16:32*

1992

I didn't plan my escape well . . . I just left. I grabbed my toothbrush, deodorant, and a T-shirt to sleep in. I knew that John would be home in a couple of hours, and all I needed was one night away to think. I left a note in the kitchen, as these were the days before everyone older than four years carried a cell phone.

> John,
> Don't worry about me. I just need a day away by myself.
> I'll be home tomorrow.
> Sheila

I wasn't sure where I'd go. I didn't have any family in Virginia Beach, and I didn't want to stay with someone from the Christian Broadcasting Network and start rumors that my marriage was falling apart. I found a small motel about an hour outside town and checked in for one night.

"Do you have any luggage?" the young guy with tattooed arms and jet-black hair at the front desk asked me.

"No," I said.

I took my key and drove to the entrance closest to my room. I climbed the two flights of metal stairs and put the plastic card into the slot in room 315. The room smelled of stale smoke and burned coffee. I sat on the edge of the bed.

Lord, I prayed silently, *I don't know what to do. I'm so afraid. I feel so lost. Please help me!*

My schedule was killing me. Monday through Friday each week I cohosted *The 700 Club* with Pat Robertson; then immediately after that show ended, I hosted my own thirty-minute show, *Heart to Heart with Sheila Walsh.* Each Friday, when my show was over, I would literally run out of the studio to catch my flight to wherever my concert was that night. Saturday morning I flew to another city for another concert, then home Sunday evening to start the treadmill all over again. I pleaded with John to let me stop traveling on weekends, but he believed if I stopped performing, I'd lose my place in the music industry. I didn't care. I was so tired and felt very alone. My life had spiraled out of control.

1981

At some point I started to realize that the women John had dated before we married were far more glamorous and confident than me. The first time his secretary met me, she said, "Gosh, you don't look like any of his usual girlfriends. He usually goes for party girls!" I think she meant it kindly, but it made me feel like an extra from *Little House on the Prairie*!

Before we married I had very romantic ideas about what our life together would be. As a twenty-six-year-old virgin, I went to see my family doctor, who'd known me since I was a child, and asked him to recommend a good book. "Don't give me something written by the Puritans in 1850," I said. "I need a good book!"

He laughed and picked out a book from his bookcase. "Don't read it all at once!" he said. "You're a Baptist; pace yourself."

So I studied that "manual of love" and asked God to help me be the kind of wife that every man longs for. I thought John would be happy that I didn't seem quite so green behind the ears on our honeymoon, but he wasn't. I think he had me on a bit of a spiritual pedestal. In his mind, I was the good girl. I was the pure girl. But I was also his wife and wanted to love and be loved like that.

I began to lose confidence in myself, as days became weeks and then months. Neither of us knew how to talk about profoundly intimate things, and as more and more time passed, it made the conversation difficult to start. I was pretty sure I was the problem. I never felt attractive growing up, and I thought that he regretted marrying me. After I met some of the women he'd dated before me, I was convinced! It started with the photographer who shot the cover for my first solo album.

When she arrived, I was blown away. She looked like a runway model, one of the most beautiful women I'd ever seen. She was tall and very slender, with dark, glossy hair and big green eyes. As she adjusted the lighting, I asked her how she and my husband knew each other.

"We dated for a while last year," she said.

I looked at her and looked at myself. Something broke in me. It wasn't just his former girlfriends that added to my insecurity; John's whole world was far more star-studded than a girl from a small town in Scotland was prepared for.

My musical hero in those days was recording artist Larry Norman, a blond, long-haired musician often referred to as the father of Christian rock music. I'd seen him in concert when I was sixteen and became a huge fan. I had all his albums and knew the lyrics to every song. So when John told me that he would be producing Larry's British tour, I couldn't wait to meet him. In the middle of his rehearsal day, Larry called and asked if I'd like to have lunch with him. I met him in the hotel restaurant and managed to say hello without falling over.

I will never forget that lunch! It was excruciatingly painful. I may have to breathe in a paper bag just to get through the retelling. I ordered lamb chops and peas . . . a meal that I've never ordered since! He ordered nothing. He just sat and watched me fruitlessly attempting to get the blooming peas onto my fork. They were flying all over the restaurant like mini green missiles. When I finally gave up, he asked me to follow him to his room. I thought of everything my mother ever told me about girls being sold into slavery. I could see the headline in the newspaper the following morning:

Chunky Scottish Girl
Trafficked by Christian Rocker

Larry asked me to stand in front of a full-length mirror and tell him what I saw.

How weird is that?!

I had no idea what to say, so I just spat out the obvious, "I see me!"

"No, that's not what I mean," he said. "Does this look like a star to you?"

"Nope," I said.

"Me neither," he responded. "We need to work on that. We'll come up with a plan."

I don't remember anything else he said. I just thanked him and left.

As I walked to the train station, I felt sick to my stomach. I didn't want to be worked on. I didn't want to be a star. I just wanted to be the woman God had called me to be; I just wasn't sure who that was.

1992

I looked at my reflection in the motel mirror. I looked older than thirty-five, with dark circles under my eyes and frown lines on my forehead. I brushed my teeth and got into bed. I fell asleep with the noise of cartoons coming through the paper-thin walls of the room next door.

I wasn't sure how long I'd been asleep when a loud banging rattled my door. Terrified, I looked at my watch. Three in the morning. I called the front desk and told him someone was at my door.

"It's okay," he said. "It's your husband. He's here to surprise you!"

My heart sank. I looked through the peephole in my door, and there John stood. I opened the door and he came in. I could tell he was angry.

"Let's go!" he said.

"It's three o'clock in the morning. Didn't you get my note?" I asked.

"I came to find you, of course!" he said. "I called every hotel I could think of."

"I just wanted one night alone—that's all," I said.

"We're going home!"

I don't believe now that John was any kind of threat to me that night. He was angry and, yes, controlling, but he just wanted to go home and go to bed and not talk about it again. But I wasn't able to tell my heart and mind that then. When someone, particularly a man, got angry with me in those days, I feared for my life. It wasn't reasonable, but it was real to me. My dad's anger when I was five *was* out of control and my life *was* in danger. I'd never had any help to understand and begin to heal from that, so when I felt threatened I became a terrified five-year-old child again. I knew that control was a huge issue for John before we were married, but rather than running for the hills, I flew closer, like a moth drawn to the flame. They say a girl marries her father; it looked as though I had become the cliché.

Perhaps you see some of that in your own life. If you grew up in a crazy house, then crazy is what's normal to you. If yelling and screaming filled your young head and heart, then often hollering becomes the soundtrack to your adult life as well. If your family was cold and non-emotional, you'll often be drawn to those traits in a partner. If your sexual purity was violated when you were a child, then sex is sometimes the first thing you offer up in a relationship because that's what's expected of you, or that's where you believe your worth is.

It feels as if the opposite should happen, but when we have unresolved issues, we gravitate to what's familiar, perhaps hoping this time we can change the ending. As humans, we long to see a finished story, so if we meet someone who reminds us of that unfinished story, we surmise that we have a second chance at completing it. Unfortunately, the story usually ends up the same exact way, with more heartache to process in the aftermath.

I saw that pattern with a family in our church in Scotland when I was in my early teens. They struggled to stay intact. The father had a terrible temper and would rage at his wife and children. When one of the daughters married, I was relieved for her and prayed that this would be the beginning of a new, peaceful, and happy life. When I heard that she had left her husband and was in a home for battered wives, I couldn't understand it at all. Why on earth would she marry someone like her dad?

Of course, I understand now and my heart aches for her. She chose what she recognized, and it almost cost her life.

It's sad to me now that I entered into a marriage that no one in my life supported. A healthy young woman would rarely do that, but I longed to control what I hadn't been able to control as a child, and John was the avenue to do that. I could do nothing as a five-year-old to defuse my father's rage or fix whatever was wrong with him. But with John, I thought I could. Even though my dad took his anger out on me, I felt intensely protective of him. I never told my mum about the beginning stages of his rage, when he would spit in my face or pull my hair out. I didn't want anyone to stop loving him. The secret only came out when his violence almost cost me my life.

So something familiar rose up in me when my friends and coworkers judged John. The protective cape I had spread over my dad, I determined to spread over him. I wanted to fix whatever was broken that had caused him to make a lot of poor choices. The reality, of course, is that I couldn't, and he didn't want to be fixed.

Control is a big issue for women. Part of it is birthed in a healthy place. We want to fashion our homes into peaceful places. We want to protect our children. We want them to know they're loved, and from that solid foundation, make good choices. If we're married, we want our husbands to succeed and feel fulfilled. We want our families and friends to love and serve God. These are all good things. But what happens when those around us don't cooperate with our efforts to control? Control moves from a healthy place to a manipulative and potentially destructive act.

✳ Your husband doesn't want to go to church, so you try to nag him into the kingdom.
✳ Your child's grades are going down at school, so you try to force him to apply himself more.
✳ You apply for a position that you know you're the most qualified for, and it goes to someone else, less qualified, so you fume and stew about it.
✳ Your Bible study leader chooses a different study than the one you made clear you believed you should all be doing next.
✳ Your church appoints a new pastor, and you don't believe he's God's man for the job.

- ✻ A new guy enters your circle of friends. You really like him, but he starts dating your friend.

What do you do when people don't act right? Seriously, think about it for a moment. How do you deal with these out-of-control situations in your life when they crop up? The above may not be the examples you relate to, but you know what your control points are.

When we long for control, we choose one of the following.

We spiritualize:

- ✻ "The only reason I'm upset is that I don't believe this is what the Lord wants!"
- ✻ "I've prayed about this for a while, and I just don't have any peace about it."
- ✻ "It's God's will that all my family would be in church together."

Feel free to add the rest . . .

We punish:

- ✻ "I think it's fine if that's what you want to do. I just can't be part of it!"
- ✻ "If you're not interested in my Jesus, then I'm not interested in coming to your company dinner!"
- ✻ "If you can't get better than a B in Math, then I don't think you need to see your friends this weekend."

Perhaps worst of all, we withdraw:

- ✻ "I won't yell and scream at you. I just won't talk at all."
- ✻ "You hurt my feelings, and until you realize what you did, I don't want to be around you."
- ✻ "I'm not coming to your baseball game. I'm staying home."

It's easy to feel quite righteous about withdrawal because yelling or screaming; we're just not "there."

Me? My weapon of choice was withdrawal. I didn't realize it then, but the more I withdrew in one situation, the more I found withdrawal spilling into other relationships and situations too. When you slam a door inside your soul to keep yourself safe, you find yourself desperately alone. You'd think it would be hard to be on national television every day or on platforms at night and hold yourself back from people, but it's actually disturbingly easy.

There is only one cure for this devastating sickness of the soul. It's a radical surrender of everything you are and have, everything you love and hold dear, to the sovereign control of God. That's not easy to do or even tempting, unless you are utterly convinced that God is good and He is for you. It's taken me a long time to come to the place where I'm no longer driven to try to grab control when I feel afraid. I had to see a lot of life rise and fall. I had to face threats that didn't seem empty. If you are as broken as I was and someone you once trusted looks right at you and says, "I will destroy you," those words ring true and fill you with terror. Mostly I had to fall on my face before God and stay there for a long time and let God do what only He can do.

"Listen carefully," Jesus said. "Unless a grain of wheat is buried in the ground, dead to the world, it is never any more than a grain of wheat. But if it is buried, it sprouts and reproduces itself many times over. In the same way, anyone who holds on to life just as it is destroys that life. But if you let it go, reckless in your love, you'll have it forever, real and eternal." (John 12:24–25 THE MESSAGE)

As my marriage began to crumble, the threats from John became more acute. In retrospect I understand that when you are hurting you can say things that you don't mean, but that didn't lessen the pain at the time.

He made it clear to me that he had the power to destroy my ministry and my music career. I'd just finished a new Christmas CD, and my vocals were taken off and the tracks given to another artist. That was just the first of many blows that left me reeling.

When someone threatens to tar and feather your name, you have two choices.

1. You can try to fight back, which will rip you both to pieces.
2. You can give up your attempts at control, let the person do his or her worst, and see what God will do.

But it's never quite that straightforward, is it? Just ask David.

After his heartbreaking farewell to Jonathan, David was utterly alone. He'd abandoned the palace, leaving behind his wife, Michal, and everything he called his own. Even though he knew he was the Lord's chosen one, anointed to be king over Israel, David did not retaliate or force his hand. He didn't try to sway others to his side; he left it alone. That speaks volumes to me about David's heart.

When we're wronged, we want people to know about it. When there is a church split, for example, the dividing one rarely leaves alone. We're afraid that leaving alone signals to people that we're admitting we were in the wrong.

But it can also mean something far greater: that we have completely surrendered control of our future to our sovereign God. When we are trying to save face in the world, we don't completely trust God to be our vindicator. But if we do trust God, we can stand on our own.

So David left it alone, which was a good thing—but then he made a very poor choice that cost some godly men and their families their lives.

Sir Walter Scott was right when he said, "Oh! what a tangled web we weave when first we practice to deceive!"[2]

David first approached Samuel for help (1 Sam. 19), and then Jonathan (1 Sam. 20). Finally he ran to the high priest, Ahimelech, in the town of Nob. When the priest saw David alone, he knew something was wrong. "Ahimelech trembled when he saw him. 'Why are you alone?' he asked. 'Why is no one with you?'" (1 Sam. 21:1).

It made no sense that David, the commander of the royal bodyguard, stood there on his own. But instead of confiding in Ahimelech, David lied. He told him that he was on a secret mission for Saul and his men would be joining him soon. He was so desperate to control an out-of-control situation that rather than wait on God for the next step, he came up with it himself.

It's so easy to do, isn't it? Seems innocent enough. David didn't have time to answer a lot of questions, so he took control out of fear.

Later David would write, "Keep me from deceitful ways; be gracious to me and teach me your law" (Ps. 119:29 NIV). But for now, he was about to learn that the desperate drive for control when we feel helpless can lead to making very poor choices—decisions that can lead to disaster.

He asked the high priest for bread and a weapon. The only sword there was Goliath's, so David took that and left—but not before being observed by someone else. We read that "Doeg the Edomite, Saul's chief herdsman, was there that day" (1 Sam. 21:7).

You never know who's watching you when you're someplace you shouldn't be or how the lie you've told will escalate. If David had allowed himself to be vulnerable, to relinquish complete control to God and trust Him with the outcome, he would have told the truth. Then the priest would have asked him to leave because his allegiance was to the king. But thinking that David was representing the king that day, Ahimelech gave David everything he asked for.

King Saul rampaged, out for David's blood. Whatever his official duties were as king over Israel, they had taken a backseat to the only thing that drove him now—killing David. Pay attention when you find yourself obsessing over one thing. It usually means you are treading on dangerous ground, losing perspective, grabbing at control.

Saul heard that David was hiding somewhere in Judah with a ragtag bunch of men. They were hardly an army. Instead they are described as men in trouble, in debt, or just plain fed up with life! It's interesting that when you are broken, other broken people come out of the woodwork to sit beside you. How you live before them will impact all your destinies. We'll see more about that in the next chapter.

When you allow jealousy full rein, you end up suspecting everything and everyone. That's what Saul did. Rather than standing tall, mentoring and encouraging his men, he began to tear them apart, even imagining that his son Jonathan stood in league with David. "Not one of you told me when my own son made a solemn pact with the son of Jesse. You're not even sorry for me. Think of it! My own son—encouraging him to kill me, as he is trying to do this very day!" (1 Sam. 22:8).

Quite a pathetic speech for a king! And there wasn't, of course, a word of truth in what Saul said to his men that day. David *wasn't* plotting to kill Saul, and neither was Jonathan. But he felt that both were conspiring against him.

Have you ever found yourself in a place like that, where you believe the whole world is against you? When we feel helpless, it's so tempting to want to attach blame and suspect even the one who is most trustworthy in your circle. The enemy of God would love for you to wallow in that place. He'd love to isolate you and make you believe that everyone is talking about you and no one is your true friend. He loves to see us paranoid.

A friend of mine told me that when she was younger she didn't speak to one of her friends for twenty years because she believed that she'd said something very damaging to her reputation. She was so devastated that instead of facing her and asking if those words were true, she just cut her off. It hurt both of them because neither left the relationship alone—they took friends with them. When they reconciled later, they both had deep regret for such a waste of years.

We can't live like that anymore, girls. We are daughters of the King. We have to hold ourselves to a different standard than our culture adheres to or even the standard of those within the church who live carelessly, forgetting who they truly are. Christ has called us to be people who speak the truth and live in the light, who openly settle our conflicts rather than withdraw and embitter ourselves. More than that, we need to come to a place where we decide this question once and for all: Do we believe that no matter what appears to be happening all around us, God is in control? Unless we believe that deep enough to impact the hardest moments in life, we will allow the enemy to make us crazy.

As Saul's soldiers and generals listened to his tirade, Doeg the Edomite spoke up. "When I was at Nob," he said, "I saw the son of Jesse talking to the priest, Ahimelech son of Ahitub. Ahimelech consulted the LORD for him. Then he gave him food and the sword of Goliath the Philistine" (1 Sam. 22:9–10).

Scripture doesn't tell us if Doeg understood the weight of his words that day or if he was just trying to curry favor with the king, but he had just signed the death warrant of not only the high priest but also eighty-four other priests who served with him.

Saul ordered the high priest to be brought to him. This humble servant of God and of King Saul was dragged in like a common criminal. When we start to suspect the most innocent among us, we are heading for a type of destructive madness.

"Why have you and the son of Jesse conspired against me?" Saul demanded. "Why did you give him food and a sword? Why have you consulted God for him? Why have you encouraged him to kill me, as he is trying to do this very day?"

"But sir," Ahimelech replied, "Is anyone among all your servants as faithful as David, your son-in-law? Why, he is the captain of your bodyguard and a highly honored member of your household! This was certainly not the first time I had consulted God for him! May the king not accuse me and my family in this matter, for I knew nothing at all of any plot against you." (1 Sam. 22:13–15)

King Saul ordered his bodyguards to kill all eighty-five of the priests of Nob, even as they stood innocent in their priestly robes. But the men refused to do such an evil thing, so Saul ordered Doeg to do it. That day he murdered not only the priests, but their wives and children too. Only one boy escaped . . . one of the high priest's sons. He ran and ran until he found David and told him about the massacre of everyone he knew and loved.

"David exclaimed, 'I knew it! When I saw Doeg the Edomite there that day, I knew he was sure to tell Saul. Now I have caused the death of all your father's family. Stay here with me, and don't be afraid. I will protect you with my own life, for the same person wants to kill us both'" (vv. 22–23).

I can't imagine how David must have felt that day, especially as a man with a tender heart toward God and others. To realize that he had inadvertently caused the deaths of so many must have been an unbearable weight to carry.

One moment of grabbing control when he felt he had to come up with a plan of his own had tragic repercussions. One domino fell and set off a devastating chain reaction that cost so many so much.

As David's sorrow turned to anger toward Doeg, a man willing to sell his soul, he wrote Psalm 52:

Why do you boast about your crimes, great warrior?
Don't you realize God's justice continues forever?

All day long you plot destruction.
  Your tongue cuts like a sharp razor;
  you're an expert at telling lies.
You love evil more than good
  and lies more than truth. Interlude

You love to destroy others with your words,
  you liar!
But God will strike you down once and for all.
  He will pull you from your home
  and uproot you from the land of the living. Interlude

The righteous will see it and be amazed.
  They will laugh and say,
"Look what happens to mighty warriors
  who do not trust in God.
They trust their wealth instead
  and grow more and more bold in their wickedness."
                                        (vv. 1–7)

David couldn't change what evil had occurred. He couldn't undo the damage he'd done. All he could do now was live differently, wiser.

It's the same for us. When we've messed up, whether we've grabbed control of a situation that we should have left alone or left something undone we should have done, we can't go back. But by God's grace we can move forward.

My dear friend Barbara Johnson profoundly lived out this truth of forward momentum. I don't think it's a coincidence that I met Barbara just a couple of weeks after that troubling night in the motel with the smell of smoke and burnt coffee.

I knew her as a bestselling author, but I'd never met her and didn't know the extent of her heartbreaking story until I met her as a guest on my television show. She didn't look like a bestselling author; she looked like my mum. She was wearing a bright-purple dress and had the same shampoo and set I've done for my mum a hundred times. When she began to talk, her story instantly captivated me.

She talked about what it was like to walk into a cold, sterile, strange-smelling room to identify her youngest son sent home from Vietnam in a body bag. At first she thought they'd got it wrong. "That's not my son!" she cried. But it was. The horrible reality was that he had been lying face-down in a rice paddy for three days and was unrecognizable as her baby boy. She lost her eldest son, too, in a devastating car crash somewhere in Canada. Once more, she had to go to the very same morgue and identify another son. I could hardly breathe as she talked. I couldn't imagine the horror of all that. But Barbara said it was a different son and a very different situation that taught her the greatest lesson about control.

As she sorted through some things in her son David's room, she came across a pile of homosexual pornography, horrifying her. This son was their golden boy, with such a bright future ahead of him. When she confronted him with what she had discovered, the conversation went very badly. He told her he'd known for some time that he was gay. She was angry and hurt and said things that she later regretted, but it was too late to take them back.

David left and she didn't see him again for seven years. Seven years is a long time to be separated from your child, particularly when you have already buried two. She didn't know where he was or if he was dead or alive.

Have you ever been in a devastating place like that?

It may be a word or an action that you can't take back.

It may be how your child is living right now, and you have no control over his or her behavior.

It may be a marriage that is broken because of something you said or did. You deeply regret your actions, you beg for forgiveness, but you have no control over whether your spouse forgives you or not.

So what do you do in the meantime?

What did David do after he was anointed king, yet remained on the run with a few disenfranchised men?

What do you do when your son is gone and you have no idea where?

What do you do when you love God but find yourself in a life that is tearing you apart?

What do you do when life feels so *out of control*?

You do what Barbara chose to do. By God's grace, you redeem the meantime, and yes, waiting can be a very "mean" time. During the years her son was gone from her life, she started a ministry called Spatula Ministries for moms who need to be scraped off the ceiling because of difficult situations with their kids! Not only that, she began to reach out to those with AIDS. Years later I asked Barbara how she survived those difficult years. She told me that when you give your heartache and pain to God and trust Him with the outcome, there is such freedom. She was most known for this phrase: "Whatever, Lord!"

Can you say that? And can you bring what feels so out of control to God, knowing He is good and He loves you, and trust Him with the timing?

We long for peace but we often grab control because it makes us feel that we are doing something. The truth is that the only place where true peace is found is in Christ, the Prince of Peace.

———— ✺ ————

I was sobbing into the carpet. I felt so out of control. A friend I'd worked with in Youth With A Mission years before in Hong Kong had just called and told me that John had phoned him and told him I'd lost my mind. I wondered how many others he'd called. Finally I picked up the phone and called Steve, a spiritual mentor who knew what was going on. He asked me one question: *"Do you believe that God is with you?"*

Such a simple question, but it changed everything. I thought I longed for the craziness to stop, but actually I longed for the peace of Christ. The peace that Jesus offers can always be found, no matter how stormy the sky is, for He is our peace.

A few weeks later, a woman I'd loved and admired for years invited me to spend a few days with her. The lessons I learned at her feet continue to impact me today.

Ruth Bell Graham, late wife of Dr. Billy Graham, was a wise and godly woman. As we sat by the fire one night, wood crackling and flame-red sparks escaping up the chimney, she opened her well-worn Bible and read these words from Paul's letter to the church at Philippi: "Be anxious for nothing, but in everything by prayer and supplication with thanksgiving let your requests be made known to God. And the peace of God, which surpasses all comprehension, will guard your hearts and your minds in Christ Jesus" (Phil. 4:6–7 NASB). She then talked about the years when her son Franklin wanted nothing to do with God. His rebellion and the choices he was making terrified her. She said, "I used to get down on my knees beside my bed with tears pouring down my cheeks, begging God to bring my prodigal home . . . until I remembered this passage. I've known it all my life, but I'd missed one word—*thanksgiving.*"

She said giving thanks shifts everything inside of us. It's us saying to God, "I don't know how You'll do this, but You are God and You do all things well, and I trust You—I let go."

Can you do that today? Can you bring the thing you long to fix to God, give it to Him, and trust Him? When we worship instead of worry, the peace of Christ will flood our hearts and minds.

FIVE

The Longing for Your Rights

"Deserves it! I daresay he does. Many that live deserve
death. And some that die deserve life. Can you give it
to them? Then do not be too eager to deal out death in
judgment. For even the very wise cannot see all ends."[1]
—*J. R. R. Tolkien, The Fellowship of the Ring*

He allowed the Ark of his might to be captured;
he surrendered his glory into enemy hands.
—*Psalm 78:61*

IN APRIL 2015 MY SON, CHRISTIAN, AND I
boarded our flight from Dallas, Texas, to Sydney, Australia. It's the
longest direct flight there is—seventeen hours. Christian is six feet tall,
so I was concerned about him being squeezed into a metal tube flying
through the air for that amount of time. I shouldn't have worried. He is
such a road warrior and has been since he was a child.

I was a guest speaker at the Colour Conference, Hillsong Church's
conference for women in Australia. I'd spoken at Colour before in London
and Kiev, but this would be my first time to visit the genesis of this
beautiful movement of women across the globe. Hillsong's impact on the
world is impressive. Pastors Brian and Bobbie Houston head up Hillsong

Church. There are now church plants in Sweden, Holland, Denmark, France, South Africa, England, Russia, Ukraine, Spain, Argentina, Brazil, and two in the United States, in New York and Los Angeles. Pastor Brian describes the movement as "one house, many rooms."

I was excited not only to speak at the conference but also to get a chance to teach at Sunday services across three of the Sydney campuses. I've loved the worship that comes from Hillsong for a long time, so to have the privilege of soaking in that atmosphere was a gift to an often road-weary heart. Tom Bachtle, one of the pastors and one of the kindest men Christian and I have ever met, picked us up at the airport and took us to our hotel in downtown Sydney, just a short walk away from the famous Sydney Opera House and Harbor Bridge.

The television in my room was on, tuned to Sky News. I reached for the remote to turn it off so I could take a nap, but I paused. The faces of two men filled the screen. Something about one of them, a man identified as Andrew Chan, drew me in. It wasn't that it was a flattering photo—far from it. A journalist had snapped it as Andrew was being taken from his prison cell into court, but I felt compelled to sit down and listen. These two Australian men, Andrew Chan and Myuran Sukumaran, had been arrested for drug smuggling in 2005, a crime punishable by death in Indonesia.

I had a sickening memory of those strictly enforced laws from a concert tour I'd taken in the late eighties to Malaysia, Indonesia, and Singapore. Before I landed in Kuala Lumpur in Malaysia, a flight attendant gave me a landing card to fill out. In bold type at the bottom it said that if I were found to be carrying any drugs, I would be hung. In Indonesia the landing card said I would be shot by firing squad. I was so genuinely freaked out that I flushed my Advil and my vitamins down the airplane toilet!

The television reporter talked about the execution date fast approaching for these two men, known as part of the Bali Nine. I prayed for them, wondering what their story was, not knowing whether they had a relationship with Christ or not.

That evening at dinner, I asked Bobbie if she knew anything about the men. Her eyes filled with tears. She told me that Brian had been in contact with Andrew and had been praying for him and encouraging him. I was so glad to know that this man whose face had captivated me knew Christ. But I wanted to know more. How did Andrew find faith on death row? Was there any hope of a reprieve?

I went online and found an article on the Bible Society's Web page. A small team from the international evangelism organization Leading the Way had been allowed to visit Andrew in 2013. What they shared was remarkable. At the time of their visit, Andrew was leading the Christian church inside Kerobokan Prison, a wretched place on the Indonesian island of Bali. He preached and led worship. He had no formal training, but he served as pastor to the other prisoners, spending his days serving Christ. Knowing it was unlikely that his death sentence would be overturned, Andrew trained leaders to carry on the work of the Lord in Kerobokan after his death.

Chris Makin from Leading the Way asked Andrew how he had come to faith. These are Andrew's words:

I found myself in here. At first I thought it was no big deal, I'll get outta this. It wasn't until I ended up in solitary confinement that I realized I wasn't going to get outta this. In fact, I figured they were gonna kill me. I had never felt so hopeless and alone before, and decided that if they were going to kill me anyway, I'd just do it myself. I took my T-shirt off and made a noose, and then remembered the heaven/hell issue, and decided that if I was gonna kill myself I should make sure I ended up in heaven. I wasn't sure how to do that, but figured I should pray. I wasn't sure how to do that either, so I looked up and just said "God[,] if you're real . . . ," and for the first time in my life I began to cry and ended up on my knees.

I cried and cried and said, "God[,] if you're real, send someone who cares about me to see me." I fell asleep like that. At 6:30 the next morning a guard woke me up. I woke up cursing him in my usual response, and he said "Get up, you've got a visitor." I said, "I can't have a visitor, no one knows I'm here." He took me to the visitor area and I saw my brother. I thought, my mum must have seen this on the news and sent my brother to see about me, because I knew my brother wouldn't just come—we don't like each other. We get along like cats and dogs.

When I got to him, he said, "Andrew, no matter what happens or how long it takes, I'm gonna be here with you." I told him to bring me a Bible. I started in Genesis when I got it and thought, "These are a lot of nice stories," but I got nothing out of it. . . .

Just before my court date, I remember reading Mark 11:23–24, where it says that if you have enough faith you can say to this mountain, "Be removed" and God will do it. So I said, "God[,] if you're real and if this is true, I want you to free me, and if you do I'll serve you every day for the rest of my life." I went to my court hearing and they convicted me and gave me the death penalty.[2]

Not the answer he was hoping for.

It may seem strange to tell Andrew's story in a chapter titled "The Longing for Your Rights." When you violate the law of the land, you surrender many of your rights.

What could Andrew possibly have in common with King David, a man who had done absolutely no wrong, who had been chosen by God to be king, with all the rights that entails, and yet was living as one already tried, convicted, and on death row?

Perhaps more pertinent: What could a convicted drug smuggler (for he had committed the crime before his conversion) have to say to you and to me on our journeys?

A lot.

It's all about freedom.

There is a mystery at play here, one that will never be understood outside of a relationship with Jesus Christ. Sadly, some of us who are followers of Christ have yet to grasp the beauty of this mystery. King Saul died by his own hand because he didn't understand or refused to submit his life to the staggering freedom that this mystery offers. King David lived by the truth of this mystery. It would sustain him through the bleakest nights and fiercest opposition, when it seemed as if his life would not be spared.

Having just received the death penalty, Andrew Chan, too, was about to be transformed by the truth of this mystery.

As he waited for his sentence to be handed down that day in court, he wondered if, now that he had a relationship with Christ, he would be saved. He was serving God, leading other prisoners into a relationship with Christ. He was a different man from the one who had broken the law ten years before. Surely God would intervene. Here are Andrew's words:

> When I got back to my cell, I said, "God, I asked you to set me free, not kill me." God spoke to me and said, "Andrew, I have set you free from the inside out, I have given you life!" From that moment on I haven't stopped worshipping Him. I had never sung before, never led worship, until Jesus set me free.

After I returned home, I followed his story. I prayed for him and the others awaiting their death sentences to be carried out. All appeals failed. The Indonesian government refused to give clemency to any of the prisoners, despite pressure from the Australian government and Amnesty International.

I sat down to write this chapter at 8:00 a.m. on April 28, 2015, knowing that in four short hours the executions would take place. There was very little about this on the news in the United States, as none of the prisoners were American, so I followed the news from Australia online. All sorts of details about their final hours were released. There is no such thing as a final meal on death row in Indonesia, but Andrew and Myuran ordered Kentucky Fried Chicken for all the Bali Nine on death row. They had been kept in separate quarters, but Andrew asked the prison governor if they could be together for their last few hours, and he agreed. A pastor who was with them said that Andrew did everything he could to encourage the others, to share Christ and the hope he had found in Him. Death row in a dreaded prison in Indonesia became a place of worship.

Andrew was executed one hour ago.

I had stopped writing for an hour before the sentence was carried out, and I'd joined with Andrew and the thousands around the world praying for and with them. I asked God that all Andrew and the others would see as they were led out to the execution field would be the face of Jesus, just as the apostle Stephen had all those years ago before they stoned him. The Bible tells us that Stephen, "full of the Holy Spirit, gazed steadily into heaven and saw the glory of God, and he saw Jesus standing in the place of honor at God's right hand. And he told [his executioners], 'Look, I see the heavens opened and the Son of Man standing in the place of honor at God's right hand!'" (Acts 7:55–56).

When the news was reported that the executions had taken place, I posted this on my Instagram page with Andrew's photo:

Then I saw a new heaven and a new earth, for the old heaven and the old earth had disappeared. And the sea was also gone. And I saw the holy city, the New Jerusalem, coming down from God out of heaven like a bride beautifully dressed for her husband. I heard a loud shout from the throne, saying, "Look,

God's home is now among his people! He will live with them, and they will be his people. God himself will be with them. He will wipe every tear from their eyes, and there will be no more death or sorrow or crying or pain. All these things are gone forever." (Revelation 21:1–4)

In the days that followed, I learned that Andrew and the others had refused the blindfolds and died with the words of "Amazing Grace" on their lips.

A moving story, right? A wonderful testimony of what God can do in the darkest places. But what does this have to do with your life right now? How does this truth fit with what we are learning about Saul and David? How does any of this relate to the things I've shared about my life?

What Andrew and King David knew deep down in the depths of their spirits will be a game-changing truth for us if we grasp hold of it. It's something that doesn't come naturally, nor does our culture encourage it—surrender. Now, when I write "surrender," I don't want you to think of yourself powerlessly waving a white flag because what you're up against is too strong and you don't think you can win. Far from it! I'm talking about an intentional, holy surrender of who you are and all you love to God because you believe that He is greater than any enemy you face now or will ever face. Your fervent prayer echoes Christ's: "Not my will but yours be done."

You may be tempted to say, "You don't know my situation!" "You don't understand what I'm facing!" "You don't know my ex-husband!" "You don't understand the lies spread about me!"

That's true, I don't. But I know what David did when given an opportunity to grab hold of his rights and defend himself. He *didn't* defend himself, even though everyone around him told him it was the right, God-ordained thing to do.

As for me, that's not such an inspiring picture. It took me a long time to "get it," and I honestly wanted to die in the process of my trouble. But let's take a look at what David did first.

We left David hiding in the cave of Adullam—along with quite a motley crew: "And when his brothers and all his father's house heard it, they went down there to him. And everyone who was in distress, and everyone who was in debt, and everyone who was bitter in soul, gathered to him. And he became commander over them. And there were with him about four hundred men" (1 Sam. 22:1–2 ESV).

David had left the palace alone. The broken and disenfranchised came *to him*. He possessed less now than when he was a shepherd boy. He didn't even have his lyre or his sheep or the simple joy of singing out under the stars and the sun. He sat in the dark, surrounded by those who were angry, disillusioned, and bitter. The word for *distress* is the Hebrew word צוק *(tsuq)*. It is used of people who are under enormous pressure. The word for *debt* here comes from the Hebrew נָשָׁה *(nashah)*. It means to have several creditors, so we're looking at people who were completely stressed-out and couldn't pay their bills. Saul was taxing people beyond what was reasonable. When they were unable to pay, he took possession of their land. They wanted justice. They knew their rights had been violated. These were men looking for a fight and longing for someone to lead it.

David refused to be that man, even when it looked as if God had delivered his enemy right into his lap: "At the place where the road passes some sheepfolds, Saul went into a cave to relieve himself. But as it happened, David and his men were hiding farther back in that very cave! 'Now's your opportunity!' David's men whispered to him. 'Today the LORD is telling you, "I will certainly put your enemy into your power, to do with as you wish" ' " (1 Sam. 24:3–4).

Try to place yourself in that cave and imagine how everyone felt. Saul had shown himself to be quite insane. He had made life miserable for those he had been anointed to lead. He'd attempted to kill David three times with his spear. He had ordered the execution of the priests and their families. Saul had given himself over to evil. In 1 Samuel 23:14 we read, "And David remained in the strongholds in the wilderness, in the hill country of the wilderness of Ziph. And Saul sought him every day, but God did not give him into his hand" (ESV). Every single day! The king of Israel, instead of pursuing kingly duties, had summoned all his men to track down David and kill him.

David cried out to the Lord for deliverance. He wrote Psalm 57 while in that very cave:

> *Have mercy on me, O God, have mercy!*
>> *I look to you for protection.*
> *I will hide beneath the shadow of your wings*
>> *until the danger passes by.*
> *I cry out to God Most High,*
>> *to God who will fulfill his purpose for me.*
> *He will send help from heaven to rescue me,*
>> *disgracing those who hound me.*
>>> (vv. 1–3)

Yet, even in his despair and darkest hour, David kept his focus on the Lord. Psalm 57 finishes like this:

> *My heart is confident in you, O God;*
>> *my heart is confident.*
>> *No wonder I can sing your praises!*
> *Wake up, my heart!*
>> *Wake up, O lyre and harp!*

I will wake the dawn with my song.
I will thank you, Lord, among all the people.
I will sing your praises among the nations.
For your unfailing love is as high as the heavens.
Your faithfulness reaches to the clouds.

Be exalted, O God, above the highest heavens.
May your glory shine over all the earth.

(vv. 7–11)

David made it clear that his heart was confident in only one thing, the Lord his God. But the men who shared the cave with him didn't see things the same way. As far as they were concerned, it was God who had delivered Saul into David's hands. Through something as basic as needing to use the bathroom, Saul had become totally vulnerable. David's men saw this as a divine opportunity and wanted to take advantage of it.

I don't think it was a coincidence that Saul picked the very cave where David and his men were hiding. God will often put us in situations to let us discover what's in us.

So what did David do? He refused the sword. Instead, he crept forward and snipped a tiny piece from the edge of King Saul's robe, then retreated again to the back of the cave. No big deal, right? Kind of quirky, actually. The kind of story you tell at a dinner party. But the act bothered David: "But then David's conscience began bothering him because he had cut Saul's robe. He said to his men, 'The LORD forbid that I should do this to my lord the king. I shouldn't attack the LORD's anointed one, for the LORD himself has chosen him" (1 Sam. 24:5–6).

I'm sure the men began to doubt David's sanity at that point! God had delivered their enemy right into their hands, and now David is bothered because he messed up the hemline of the king's robe? That wasn't the point though. David knew that even a tiny step of disobedience matters. His reverence for God was so acute that even to touch, to dese-crate, the hem of the robe of the man God had chosen, was wrong.

It's easy to justify small things. David didn't kill Saul. All he did was take a souvenir. But it tells us a lot about David's heart that even a small thing bothered him. This is a profoundly important spiritual prin-ciple that Christ echoed: "If you are faithful in little things, you will be faithful in large ones. But if you are dishonest in little things, you won't be honest with greater responsibilities" (Luke 16:10).

David chose not to fight for his rights, no matter how right they were. He trusted God alone for deliverance. Saul was in the wrong, but David wasn't going to make it his job to make it right. He would leave that task to God.

That's a hard one. If someone has done something to damage your reputation, everything inside rises up to right that wrong.

I know, for I've been in that place.

———— ✺ ————

I'm not going to go into all the reasons why I finally divorced John. I had biblical grounds that were known to our counselor and pastor. Still, I believe that a married couple committed to God and each other can survive infidelity—it's painful but survivable. Unfortunately, it was a lot more complicated than that.

So when it finally became clear to me, to my family, and to my pastor that there was no other way, John, understandably, was very angry. He had lots of friends in the music industry, so it wasn't hard to imagine a scenario where he would do as much damage to me as possible. Whatever had been broken in me up until that point shattered completely.

As a result of his love and honor for God, David didn't fight back. I didn't fight back because inside I was a scared little girl.

I stood at the end of our boat dock, thinking how easy it would be to just quietly slip into the water. I believed that a dead Sheila Walsh would be easier to handle in the Christian community than a divorced one. What stopped me was the thought of my mum receiving another phone call telling her that someone she loved had disappeared under the water. I couldn't do that to her. Instead I ended up in a psychiatric hospital. That place became my cave of sorts, where in the quiet and the dark, I could press into God. I wrote in my journal on the first night, "I never knew You lived so close to the floor."

In my "cave" I met a lot of stressed-out, spent, disenfranchised believers who, like me, had stuffed their feelings for so long they were ready to explode.

There was a missionary who had been sexually abused at seven and felt so guilty about it that she chose to serve God overseas to show how penitent she was. She hated her job. Inside she was full of rage for the injustice in her life. She was angry with God and angry at herself because she felt she had abandoned that little girl she had once been— that innocent little girl.

There was a darling young woman who had slit her wrists because no one believed her story of what had been done to her by a trusted family member.

There was a successful businessman who had finally collapsed under the weight of the lack of love from his mother when he was a little boy. "No matter how successful I am, all I hear deep inside is, 'I wish you'd never been born!'"

The outrageous inequality of life had driven many to the point of breaking. There are many things in life that are not fair. But some are so unfair the burden is too heavy to carry.

My therapist asked me one morning as I sat with my head in my hands, sobbing so hard I could barely breathe, "What's the worst your husband can do to you?"

I sat up and looked at him in disbelief. When I had composed myself enough to talk, I asked, "You want me to go there? You're supposed to be helping me!"

"Until you make peace with that, you will never be free," he said quietly.

"But it's not fair!" I cried.

Even as the words were barely off my lips, I thought back to something I'd said to a guest on a show a few weeks before. A verbally abusive mother who took great pleasure in tearing her daughter to shreds had raised her. I was deeply moved as I listened to this woman describe how finding a relationship with Christ had transformed everything.

"I used to want to see her suffer for the pain she'd caused, but after being saved and loved by God, I didn't need that anymore."

As I wrapped the show that day, I said, "One thing has become very clear to me today: fair doesn't live here, but Jesus does."

Now these words came back to me. I felt their weight.

Fair doesn't live here, but Jesus does.

Something shifted in me that day. I'd been a Christian since I was eleven, but now I began to read the Word of God with new eyes and a fresh hunger. Words that I had read before became alive in me. Like these: "I tell you the truth, unless a kernel of wheat is planted in the soil and dies, it remains alone. But its death will produce many new kernels—a plentiful harvest of new lives. Those who love their life in this world will lose it. Those who care nothing for their life in this world will keep it for eternity" (John 12:2–25).

I thought, *What does it matter if everything falls apart? Let it go. Let the whole thing go. Christ will remain, and He is all I need.*

I remembered the verse I was given when I was baptized at sixteen. "You didn't choose me. I chose you. I appointed you to go and produce lasting fruit, so that the Father will give you whatever you ask for, using my name" (John 15:16).

I rested in the promise that it was God who chose me and that whatever fruit my life had produced that was of Him would last, and everything else could fall to the ground.

I sat with those life-giving words for a long time. And I began to take comfort in some basic truths:

* So what if your ministry falls into the ground and dies? God still loves you!
* So what if you never make another record or sing another song or write another book? That won't change the course of world history!
* Sheila, do you believe that God is good and He is in control? Yes, I do!
* Have you made anyone more powerful than God in your life? Yes, I have!

I spent a month in that hospital. A psych ward was one of God's greatest gifts to me. Just as He did for Andrew Chan, sometimes God will take you to prison to set you free.

A few years later I bumped into John in California, where I attended seminary. We sat down and had lunch. He showed me pictures of his beautiful new wife. He was very proud of her. I was very happy for him. He asked me about Women of Faith, an organization I'd been speaking with since 1996. I told him the ministry had been a perfect fit. All the speakers had found the most profound relationship with Christ in the darkest caves of their lives. The love of God shone through our brokenness.

"The thing I love most," I said, "is that Christ is the hero of all our stories. It was quite a relief to discover that I'm not the good news; He is!"

I asked him to forgive me for any way that I had contributed to the breakdown of our lives. God had made it clear to me as I sat listening to him that I should do that without the slightest hesitation or expectation.

When we parted ways he hugged me and said, "I knew you'd be fine!" As I watched him walk away, I prayed the grace and mercy and love of God would crash over him in waves. We all need a tidal wave of His love. John taught me we are all broken.

David held his men back that day in the cave from acting on the murder in their hearts. He owed them no explanation because the person he'd wronged was King Saul.

> After Saul had left the cave and gone on his way, David came out and shouted after him, "My lord the king!" And when Saul looked around, David bowed low before him. Then he shouted to Saul, "Why do you listen to the people who say I am trying to harm you? This very day you can see with your own eyes it isn't true. For the LORD placed you at my mercy back there in the cave. Some of my men told me to kill you, but I spared you. For I said, 'I will never harm the king—he is the LORD's anointed one.' Look, my father, at what I have in my hand. It is a piece of the hem of your robe! I cut it off, but I didn't kill you. This proves that I am not trying to harm you and that I have not sinned against you, even though you have been hunting for me to kill me." (1 Sam. 24:7–11)

Saul wept as he listened to David. For a moment his heart softened, and the dark mist he'd cultivated in his soul cleared enough for him to see the truth. He acknowledged that he knew David would be king. Then he made a request. "Now swear to me by the LORD that when that happens you will not kill my family and destroy my line of descendants!" (1 Sam. 24:21).

David promised. It was a promise he would keep in one of the most profound lessons in grace we find in Scripture. We will look at that in chapter 9.

For now, dear sister, I want to sit with you for a moment.

Are there places where you need to surrender to God? Are there people you need to give to God? Have there been bitter tears because life is so unfair?

Are you telling your story over and over because there's been no justice for you?

Believe me; I understand. I would ask you one thing though: to sit quietly for a moment and reflect on the sacrifice Christ made for you. The innocent Lamb of God was brutally tortured and murdered in a place of shame with common criminals because He loves you so much. Now, can you imagine yourself kneeling at the foot of that cross, pointing a finger at someone else? No matter how brutal your story is—there is One who understands the depth of your pain and grief and offers to carry it for you. He offers a beautiful exchange: "Come to me, all of you who are weary and carry heavy burdens, and I will give you rest. Take my yoke upon you. Let me teach you, because I am humble and gentle at heart, and you will find rest for your souls. For my yoke is easy to bear, and the burden I give you is light" (Matt. 11:28–30).

Rest here for a while. There is healing for your maligned soul. I understand the deep longing to be understood, to stand up for yourself, and to right the wrongs, but it's an exhausting process that only prolongs the pain.

In the weeks, months, and years that followed my divorce, many people wanted to know the ins and outs of everything that had taken place in my marriage. I decided to say nothing. My pastor, family, and closest friends knew, and that was enough for me. I had magazines and newspapers contact me, offering to let me tell my side of the story. How ridiculous is that! As daughters of the King, our allegiance is to Him and to rest in the protective shadow of His wings. There is such an unhealthy thirst in our culture and in the church to know all the details of someone's pain and brokenness, but life is not a spectator sport. It's to be lived in vulnerability and truth and community. That is where we surrender our right to be "right." I realized I didn't need everyone there to understand or approve. I found joy in being loved by Him!

For Andrew, when that fatal shot was fired, he entered immediately into the presence of Christ his Savior. He had longed to be set free on this earth but was given a far greater freedom, one that no one could touch. His real life has begun.

For me, I decided just to disappear for a while. Some were kind enough to offer to work to help put my ministry back together and to counter any false rumors that were circulating about me, but I said no. At one point I longed for that, but the more I searched my heart, the more crystal clear it became that it was not what I wanted. I have no "rights" as a believer. I am a sinner saved by grace, called to live a surrendered life.

I went back to seminary, this time in California at Fuller Seminary. I didn't want business as usual. I wanted to dig deep into my faith and press deeper into my Father's love. When we have been wounded or wronged, we can fight, we can run, or we can hide. I chose to hide! "Those who live in the shelter of the Most High will find rest in the shadow of the Almighty," David wrote.

> *This I declare about the LORD:*
> *He alone is my refuge, my place of safety;*
> *he is my God, and I trust him."*
>
> (Ps. 91:1–2)

So I think about you, dear sister. Are you being eaten up inside with the brutal inequity of life? Do you long as David did to explain, "I could have hurt you and I chose not to"? Are you desperate to tell your side of a broken story? I want you to know that God is far more capable of handling your reputation than you are—in His time and in His way. As I sit at my desk today in Dallas, Texas, and reflect over the last decades and the privilege of speaking to more than five million women, I marvel at the mercy and grace of God.

This truth is hard to grasp, but you can stake your life on it: even when everything seems a mess, you can press your face into the mane of the Lion of Judah and trust Him. Our God is sovereign.

SIX

The Longing for That One Thing
You Think You Need to Be Happy

I think everybody should get rich and famous
and do everything they ever dreamed of so
they can see that it's not the answer.
—*Jim Carrey*

"But seek (aim at and strive after) first of all His
kingdom and His righteousness (His way of
doing and being right), and then all these things
taken together will be given you besides."
—*Matthew 6:33* AMP

I WAS RANDOMLY PERUSING THE INTERNET ONE
day and decided to Google my last name. The name Walsh is rare here in
America. Now, if you ever visit Dublin, Ireland, which I highly recommend, you will fall over Walshes on every street corner. But in the states,
the Walsh clan is a small, select breed. My online search did produce an
interesting story, though, about a Bill Walsh, an Illinois scientist.

In 2000, he conducted chemical tests on a few strands of hair from
the great German composer Ludwig van Beethoven. The article didn't say

how he got hold of these hairs; after all, Beethoven died in 1827. Perhaps they were bequeathed to him from his great-aunt Helga? Anyway, upon Beethoven's death, several family members and friends had taken clippings of his hair. (Note to self: leave note for family members stating that on the event of my untimely demise, people with scissors should be banned from the viewing!)

What Bill discovered was fascinating. Apparently Beethoven's body had a hundred times the normal amount of lead that a human being should have. The original autopsy had revealed significant liver damage, so it was assumed that he died due to heavy alcohol consumption. But Bill Walsh concluded that it's far more likely that Beethoven's death at age fifty-six was the result of lead poisoning. How that occurred is bitterly ironic.

Beethoven had been in poor health for years, so his doctor had recommended he spend as much time as possible at a mineral spa. He loved the mineral water and mineral baths. But it's now believed that he died slowly from lead poisoning from the very place he believed would bring health and healing. How could he have known that the health he longed for would lead to his death?

Unfortunately, many of our appetites have similar devastating consequences.

I received an anonymous letter a few months ago. The author finished her letter by saying that if her story might help another woman, I could share it. In that spirit I'll share a portion, asking only that you would pray for her.

My marriage had been in trouble for a while. My husband was always busy, working overtime and sometimes weekends. He said it was to pay down our mortgage so we could take things a bit easier later. He was always tired. We rarely had sex. He hardly even kissed me anymore. I'm sure you can tell what's coming but it didn't feel like that. It was a guy at our church. He's married, too, but he told me he didn't love her. At first it was just flirting, then we went for coffee after a thing at church. I couldn't wait to see him again. When he suggested I meet him at a motel I knew what I was doing but I thought we were in love. After we had sex a few times I told him I loved him. I thought he felt the same way. He told me he loved his wife. I was so angry that I called her and told her. She called my husband. I've lost everything. He went back to his wife but my husband won't forgive me. I just want my life back.[1]

My heart aches for this woman. What she longed for was to be seen and to be loved, but the quick fix she chose proved to be catastrophic. In other parts of her letter, she talked about how she used to be very involved in her church, but she'd pulled away from some of the ministries. That was dangerous ground. When we separate ourselves from those who remind us of who we are at our core and what's true no matter what we might feel at the moment, that's precisely the moment when the enemy is able to stalk us and take us down.

Peter warned of this. "Stay alert! Watch out for your great enemy, the devil. He prowls around like a roaring lion, looking for someone to devour. Stand firm against him, and be strong in your faith" (1 Peter 5:8–9). The Greek word used here for "devour" is the same word used in Hebrew in Jonah 1:17 for the great fish that "swallowed" Jonah whole. The enemy wants to eat us. When we separate ourselves from our tribe, our people, we just make his job that much easier. Personal isolation is one of the most tragic lessons from King David's life. At the point when he should have been his strongest, David's sexual passions led him down a path of destruction. His choices also devastated the lives of others, because sin is a path few of us ever take alone.

"In the spring of the year, when kings normally go out to war, David sent Joab and the Israelite army to fight the Ammonites. They destroyed the Ammonite army and laid siege to the city of Rabbah. However, David stayed behind in Jerusalem" (2 Sam. 11:1). Clearly to make a point, the text reads, "when kings normally go out to war," followed up by, "David stayed behind in Jerusalem." This is a different David from the boy who had chased Goliath. David was the great warrior king. The people hailed him as a killer of ten thousands. So what happened? Whatever it was, lethargy didn't happen overnight. Sin rarely does.

James reminds us of how sin creeps in slowly, and the more room we give it, the more space it demands. "And remember, when you are being tempted, do not say, 'God is tempting me.' God is never tempted to do wrong, and he never tempts anyone else. Temptation comes from our own desires, which entice us and drag us away. These desires give birth to sinful actions. And when sin is allowed to grow, it gives birth to death" (James 1:13–15).

But we've jumped ahead quite a bit in David's story, so let's do a little catch-up.

David was about seventeen when Samuel anointed him. For a brief time, the boy returned to his flock. Then came the turning point, when he killed Goliath and went to King Saul's palace. As you remember, those glory days were short-lived. Soon David had to run for his life. He fled for thirteen years before Saul died. Thirteen years is a long time to wonder when God would intervene and do the thing He's promised. Thirteen years as an outcast, with no home, constantly watching his back because he was a marked man.

David finally received the news that King Saul had died. In a tragic end to his life, he had thrown himself on his own sword. Now it looked as if the way was finally clear for David to claim the throne of Israel.

But David didn't immediately march into Jerusalem. Those years in dark, lonely places and on foreign soil had only deepened his relationship with God and finely tuned his heart and ears to listen for God's voice. Instead, David asked God what to do.

"Should I move back to one of the towns of Judah?"

"Yes," the LORD replied.

Then David asked, "Which town should I go to?"

"To Hebron," the LORD answered.

(2 Sam. 2:1)

So David and his men went to Hebron, about twenty miles south of Jerusalem. For seven and a half years, he stayed there with a limited reign over Judah alone. David was content to stay where God told him to stay for as long as it took.

Finally all the elders of Israel came to David in Hebron and made him king over all of Israel. Catch that: twenty years from the promise until the fulfillment.

Once David became king, everything flourished under his leadership. He expanded Israel's boundaries tenfold, from six thousand square miles to sixty thousand. At last the people saw the fulfillment of the Lord's promise to Abraham, when He said, "I have given this land to your descendants, all the way from the border of Egypt to the great Euphrates River" (Gen. 15:18).

David opened new trade routes, so Israel became the most prosperous it had ever been. But prosperity wasn't enough for David because when you give free rein to your desires, they'll never be enough. Ask any woman who has become addicted to shopping. It starts out innocently enough, "Just one more pair of shoes." Then it can get so out of hand, leading to all sorts of covering up and deception. Ask anyone who has lost control over how much she eats. It began as a simple daily choice, yet turned into a food addiction. Ask any man who's become addicted to pornography to chart his course; he'll tell you he never imagined he'd become an addict. For all these it started out with early exposure, then addiction, and finally, escalation, when they needed more and more to produce the same high they got when they began. It's the same with all unfettered appetites.

David may have been content to wait on God during those seven and a half years in Hebron, but he also made some bad choices. He added five more wives to the one he had. David was a passionate man. This was his strength, but it was also his Achilles' heel. For David, when he added the one thing he believed he needed to make him happy—a woman—it led to disaster.

Once he was king in Jerusalem, he added more women to his circle. His numerous wives and concubines produced twenty sons and one daughter. Did David forget the instructions of Moses, or just think that he was above them?

When the Israelites finally reached the promised land after leaving Egypt, Moses had told them, "You are about to enter the land the LORD your God is giving you. When you take it over and settle there . . . be sure to select as king the man the LORD your God chooses. . . . The king must not take many wives for himself, because they will turn his heart away from the LORD" (Deut. 17:14–15, 17).

The king must not take many wives for himself, because they would turn his heart away from the Lord. The command is not ambiguous, is it? It's pretty straightforward. Perhaps if David had given his whole heart to one woman, he would not have been tempted that day when he decided to stay home from war. Perhaps if he had loved her and their children, his home would not have been a place where rebellion festered. David was the greatest king Israel would ever have, but God's Word records that he failed in his role as a husband and father. In the years to come, all David's trouble would be the direct result of, first, taking another man's wife, and second, his rebellious and undisciplined sons.

Fast-forward a little. David ruled in Hebron for nearly eight years.

He had reigned as king over all of Israel for almost thirteen by the time we reach 2 Samuel 11. At that point he was about fifty.

The scene: a time of peace for Israel. That should have been a good thing. Israel had fought so many battles and conquered vast amounts of territory. David was a warrior, but even with their age-old enemy the Philistines lurking nearby, they had experienced peace for a time. David had idle time on his hands.

Sometimes when we're not actively moving in our gift, we get restless. David did. As he sat around in his magnificent palace, it began to bother David that he lived in a palace but the Ark of the Lord was in a tent. He summoned Nathan the prophet and told him that he intended to build a temple for the Lord. The prophet told him to go ahead, as God was with him. But that night God spoke to Nathan and told him to tell David that he was not the man to build the temple. God had chosen another.

For David, God's no wasn't an issue of sin; it was one of calling. David was an amazing warrior king. Warring was his strength. But because of the violence of war, he would not be allowed to build the temple. In 1 Chronicles 28:2–3 he reported, "It was my desire to build a Temple where the Ark of the Lord's Covenant, God's footstool, could rest permanently. I made the necessary preparations for building it, but God said to me, 'You must not build a Temple to honor my name, for you are a warrior and have shed much blood.'" His son, he was told, would be the one to build God's house.

So David accepted God's will, but it seems he lost vision for his true calling. When the time came for a battle, he sent Joab off to fight in his stead while he went back to bed. If David had been performing what he was uniquely called and equipped to do, he would never have been on his roof one night, watching another man's wife take a bath. The David we've come to know and love would be leading the charge in war, fueled by his passion for God and hatred for the enemies of the Lord.

David never refused to go into battle while his enemy, Saul, hunted him. So long as someone stalked him like a wild animal, David's character remained spotless, and his passion was fierce.

But that same heart lost its edge. David drifted. And there's a difference between taking a break to refresh and recharge and starting to carelessly drift.

As Irish orator Edmund Burke allegedly wrote, "All that is necessary for the triumph of evil is that good men do nothing."

David wasn't looking for evil; he just wasn't living where he should have been. Those empty, unguarded hours gave space for evil to make its enticing proposition in the form of a bathing woman.

―――――∞∞∞―――――

I interviewed Dr. Billy Graham at his home in Montreat, North Carolina, on his seventieth birthday. One of the questions I asked was if he had any plans in place to retire. With his characteristic steely gaze, he said, "I can find no scriptural precedence for retirement. I will do what God has called me to do until He calls me home."

Doing nothing is dangerous to our spiritual lives. If we are not advancing the kingdom of God, then we are retreating into ourselves. We can rest for a while and allow all that God has deposited in us to take root, but when we continually neglect our spiritual purpose, we welcome weeds to choke the good seeds.

It's the same principle at work in relationships. If you ignore them, they suffer. I've heard many women talk about how hard marriage is when their kids go off to college. Suddenly it's just the husband and wife staring at each other across the cereal box. What we give time and attention to will thrive, and what we ignore suffers.

There is quite a lesson in this story by an unknown author. It is called "The Eagle and the Wolf":

There is a great battle that rages inside me.

One side is a soaring eagle. Everything the eagle stands for is good and true and beautiful. It soars above the clouds. Even though it dips down into the valleys, it lays its eggs on the mountaintops.

The other side of me is a howling wolf. And that raging, howling wolf represents the worst that is in me. He eats upon my downfalls and justifies himself by his presence in the pack.

Who wins this great battle?

The one I feed.[2]

⸺⸺⸺

In his study on the life of King David, Chuck Swindoll wrote, "David, being a man with a strong sexual appetite, mistakenly thought, *To satisfy it I will have more women.* Thus, when he became king, he added to the harem, but his drive only increased. One of the lies of our secular society is that if you just satisfy this drive, it'll be abated."[3]

David was bored, restless, and tired from not doing anything.

Late one afternoon, after his midday rest, David got out of bed and was walking on the roof of the palace. As he looked out over the city, he noticed a woman of unusual beauty taking a bath. He sent someone to find out who she was, and he was told, "She is Bathsheba, the daughter of Eliam and the wife of Uriah the Hittite." Then David sent messengers to get her; and when she came to the palace, he slept with her. (2 Sam. 11:2–4)

The shocking thing about this passage is how easy falling into sin was. That's the thing about sin. When your guard is down, the unthinkable becomes doable. David was a godly man, a man who time after time had refused to step outside the plan of God for his life, no matter what it cost him personally. He had spent years in caves and fields, hungry and at times all alone, and yet stayed true. But now things in his life were easy. He saw no perceivable enemy, so now his real enemy showed up.

In his book *Temptation*, German pastor Dietrich Bonhoeffer wrote that when any of us are faced with temptation, whether it's sexual or ambition or vanity or desire for revenge, "at this moment God is quite unreal to us. Satan does not here fill us with hatred of God, but with forgetfulness of God."[4] We see that forgetfulness here as David sends a servant to find out about the beautiful woman on the rooftop.

Note the quietly veiled warning in the report brought back to David: "She is Bathsheba, the daughter of Eliam and the wife of Uriah the Hittite." In those days, when you inquired about someone, people would tell you the name of the person and his or her father, sometimes even the person's grandfather, but never the spouse. But the servant David asked about this woman knew his master well and was trying to warn him.

Uriah wasn't simply a soldier in David's army. He was one of "the Thirty," an elite squad, the best of the best in military terms (see 2 Sam. 23:8–39). At times they served as the king's bodyguard. David knew and depended on this loyal man, but that didn't stop his plan. At that moment all he knew was this: he wanted Bathsheba, so he took her.

There's a profound warning for us here. It's easy to sit in the comfort of our lives and think, *Well, I'd never do that!* I believe every single one of us is capable of the most blatant sin given the right set of circumstances. The only thing that will save us in a moment like that is to turn around and run from it with everything that's in us. Don't walk. Run!

"Run from sexual sin!" the apostle Paul wrote. "No other sin so clearly affects the body as this one does. For sexual immorality is a sin against your own body" (1 Cor. 6:18).

The enemy never tells us the whole story when we're faced with the most luscious temptation. He entices just enough to get us hooked. He didn't tell my friend who wrote the anonymous letter that her whole life would fall apart because her lover would return to his wife. And he didn't tell David that in no time at all Bathsheba would send word that she was pregnant.

So often what we think will make us happy brings nothing but heartache. In light of impending heartache, what would David do now?

He had two choices: He could own what he did—fall on his face before God and ask for forgiveness and confess his sin to Uriah and ask him to forgive him for his one-night stand.

Or, he could cover up the affair.

That's the option David chose. And life would only get worse from that point on. Why? Because panic is a poor decision maker.

David didn't think twice about sleeping with Bathsheba. But once he learned she was pregnant, he had no desire to get caught, so he sent for Uriah. His plan was to bring Uriah home from battle for a night, anticipating that he would sleep with his wife and then assume the child was his. But David underestimated Uriah. This was not a common soldier or an ordinary man. He had served David since the early days when David ran from Saul. Although he was a Hittite by birth, his parents had probably converted to Judaism since the name Uriah means "My light is the Lord."

Uriah still considered himself to be in battle mode, so he refused to go home. Instead, he slept at the door of King David's house with the servants. When David questioned him the following morning, Uriah replied, "The Ark and the armies of Israel and Judah are living in tents, and Joab and my master's men are camping in the open fields. How could I go home to wine and dine and sleep with my wife? I swear that I would never do such a thing" (2 Sam. 11:11).

David might have stolen Uriah's wife, but he couldn't manipulate Uriah's heart.

From this point, the story takes a dark and somber twist. Realizing that he couldn't bend this godly man to his will, David determined to kill him. He sent Uriah back to the battle with a note for Joab, the commander of Israel's army. "Station Uriah on the front lines where the battle is fiercest," he wrote. "Then pull back so that he will be killed" (2 Sam. 11:15).

He made Uriah carry his own death warrant.

What David didn't know was that he had just handed Joab the perfect ammunition for blackmail. He would live to regret this murderous deception for so many reasons. Joab was just one of them.

David's plan worked. So, he got what he thought he needed to make him happy. He went after what he longed for: Bathsheba. And now, with Uriah dead, he could have her free and clear, and no one would be the wiser.

Think about this for a moment. What David did, apart from being evil, made no sense. If Uriah had come back from battle and discovered his wife was pregnant, why would he have suspected David? When we panic and try to cover up our steps, we open ourselves to crazy thinking. Telling the cold, hard truth when we've deliberately sinned is hard to do, but it is so much better than the wall of lies we build to try to cover ourselves. Why? Because those walls always fall on us. We wrongly think the truth will destroy us. It may hurt us in the short term, but it won't destroy us. That's the territory of the enemy.

1992

I sat across from my husband in a small café on the oceanfront in Virginia Beach. I'd been out of the psychiatric hospital for a few weeks and felt very fragile. I could see he was torn as to whether he should tell me some things or not. A pastor friend said he must, and his best friend told him not to. He finally confessed a past relationship.

I asked him if he had been in love with this woman.

"Of course not!" he said.

"Then why?"

"She was there."

I remember her showing up at our door one night, drunk, screaming at him. He had taken her by the arm and led her outside, telling me to stay in the house. Then he'd driven her home. When I'd asked what was going on, he'd dismissed it then. Now he told me she'd been helping him market one of his artists. But she was out of control.

"I asked you to tell me the truth years ago," I said. "You told me I was crazy for asking about her. I thought I might be."

Years of lies and denial had built a wall a mile high. Tears ran down my face and dripped onto my half-eaten sandwich. It was a desperately sad day for both of us.

When you try to cover your sin, you're trusting in your own ability to pull it off. When you throw yourself on the mercy of God, you're counting on Him to redeem you. Would it have damaged our relationship if I'd known the truth years before? Yes. But perhaps, by God's grace, we could have sought help. We both needed it desperately. It's easy to look at one person in a broken marriage and attribute blame, but that's never an accurate picture of reality.

In the years after our divorce, I discovered that there's a scale of justice meted out by some in the church based solely on one question: "Did you have scriptural grounds for divorce?" In other words, did you sin or did he?

Don't misunderstand me here. I know that God's Word is clear about sexual sin and the consequence of sex outside a marriage, but if that's the only verse we bring to the table, we have missed the heart of the gospel. The theme that runs through the Bible from Genesis to Revelation is the broken, sinful nature of men and women and the redemptive mercy of God. That's why for twenty years I've refused to talk publicly about my first marriage. It would be so easy to make myself look good and John bad. Yet God knows there were so many ways I failed to be the wife he longed for too.

I remember the moment when I heard that our divorce was final. I was at a conference in Anaheim, California, when I got a message to call the mediating attorney from our church. "It's over, Sheila. You're free," he said.

I ran upstairs to my bedroom on the second floor of the hotel. I made it to the bathroom just in time. I threw up over and over and over until there was nothing left but the bitter bile of sorrow. I had fought everyone who loved me to marry this man, believing it was the one thing I needed to make me happy, to heal me, to heal him, and now we were both more bloodied than when we began.

Perhaps you are there now. What do you do when that one thing you longed for because you thought it would make you happy turns on you like a venom-filled snake? Is your life over? Have you ruined God's plan?

Far from it.

David was about to be confronted by the prophet Nathan to have his sin exposed, cut open like the excising of a festering wound so that healing could come.

Christ meets us in our sin but He never leaves us there. Peter, one of Jesus' closest friends, betrayed Him when Jesus needed him most. That didn't change the role that Christ had chosen Peter for. Instead, Peter's sin and the grace and forgiveness he received changed him. "Now repent of your sins and turn to God, so that your sins may be wiped away," Peter preached after the Ascension. "Then times of refreshment will come from the presence of the LORD, and he will again send you Jesus, your appointed Messiah" (Acts 3:19–20).

That is our glorious hope.

This makes me think of Miranda (name changed for privacy). The first time we met she told me, "I'm going to be up on that stage with you one day soon!" I told her I'd scoot over and make room. But the next time we met there was a different look in her eyes and a weight on her shoulders. I had thirty minutes before my next teaching session, so I asked her to come back to the green room with me for a quick cup of coffee. (Green rooms are where people gather before appearing on a platform—and they are never green!)

I asked her what had happened to her.

"All I've ever wanted is to be on the platform," she told me. "I want to do what you do. I want to share my story and teach and help other women get closer to God. I knew that would make me happy, give my life some real purpose. It just was taking too long so I was sure that it was the enemy trying to stop me from being obedient. So I stepped out in faith.

"I went to a conference that was taking place in a city near mine and sat as close to the front as I could. I knew the woman who was in charge, so I asked her if it would be possible for me to have ten minutes to share a testimony of God's goodness. She wasn't sure at first, but then she said I could have five, as they had a packed schedule."

"It was a disaster," she confessed. "I've shared my story over and over in my bedroom in front of my mirror, but when I got up in front of all those women, I just froze. Then I started to cry. It was horrible. Finally the emcee came up and stood beside me and asked all the ladies to pray for me, and someone escorted me offstage. I feel like such a fool." She put her head in her hands and wept as I knelt beside her.

"Miranda," I said, "perhaps you just missed the timing. When God places a desire in our hearts, we need to trust Him for the 'when.' If God has something for you, He will never be too late or too early, just perfectly on time. Perhaps one day you'll share what you just shared with me and be able to laugh about it. But if that never happens, true joy and peace and fulfillment come from being loved by Him."

Perhaps you are in an "if only" place. You think, *If only I could have this one thing, be loved by this one person, be given this one opportunity, then I'd be happy.* But the longings we have in the depth of our beings are never satisfied long term by that one thing we believe we need. True contentment and rest come from Christ.

He alone can fill the deepest longings of our hearts.

SEVEN

The Longing to Make Everything Right

But with the morning cool repentance came.[1]
—*Sir Walter Scott, Rob Roy*

When I refused to confess my sin,
    my body wasted away,
    and I groaned all day long.
Day and night your hand of discipline was heavy
    on me.
My strength evaporated like water in the
    summer heat.
        —*Psalm 32:3–4*

SO . . . HERE IS ONE OF LIFE'S BIG QUESTIONS: Are you a dog person or a cat person?

You're allowed to love both, of course, but usually your heart's true allegiance will rest firmly in one furry camp.

I'm a dog person through and through. Now, I like cats—I've had several over my lifetime—but dogs and me, well . . . we just get each other. My dad bought me my first dog when I was four. She was a black-and-tan dachshund named Heidi. She peed every time someone rang our doorbell, a trait I found very entertaining as a child. Sadly, as the repercussions from dad's brain injury became more severe, Mum took Heidi back to the farm where she was born. It was just too much work for her with three young children as well.

I didn't have another dog until I moved to the United States. Then I had a West Highland white terrier called Charlie. Then I had another Westie called . . . Charlie. (Some days I have the creativity of a used tea bag.)

Now we have three dogs. If you follow me on Twitter or Instagram, I'm sure you're painfully aware of that fact. Belle and Tink are bichons, and Maggie is a Yorkie.

We got Belle when Christian was six. She's a very sweet dog. Her only unfortunate trait is that she thinks everyone on television is actually in our house and feels obliged to greet them. She has an exhausting life.

Tink is eight years old, and please do not judge me, but she's from Paris, France. I discovered that a woman in Pennsylvania takes a trip twice a year to a breeder in Paris and brings back small French bichon frise puppies to the United States, so we got Tink and, yes, she has her own passport, ooh la la. We bought her when we had more money than sense. That situation has now changed, but I'll tell you about that later. I realize I'm about to sink to the level of national stereotypes, but Tink is very French! She is extremely picky about her food and will not let you pet her unless she's in the mood. She's rarely in the mood.

Then we got Maggie!

"Why did you get another dog?" you might be tempted to ask.

Because my life was crazy busy and I thought a hyper barking puppy would help!

I'm sorry, people . . . it's all I've got!

When we got Maggie, the breeder recommended that we crate train her. I think in retrospect that would have been a brilliant idea, but I had a hard time putting her in a crate when the other two sleep on our bed. Most of the time Maggie remembers that our house is not a giant toilet, but every now and then she sneaks off and comes back looking relieved.

In the early spring of 2015, we put our house up for sale. Christian was about to graduate and we wanted to downsize. Our Realtor gave us a few ideas of things to do to make our home more appealing. Most of the downstairs is hardwood, but she recommended having the carpet in our bedroom cleaned, so I booked a local company to come and take care of it.

When the carpet-cleaning dude arrived and saw that we had dogs, he suggested that he do a special procedure first to take care of pet stains. I assured them that our dogs behave like little ladies and I didn't think that would be necessary. He looked at me with a mixture of pity and authority. That's when he produced the big gun!

"What is that?" I asked.

"Ma'am, this is a UV Black Light Flashlight Urine Detector," he replied with the weight of someone unveiling a new weapon of mass destruction.

I put the dogs in the laundry room and showed him into our bedroom.

"Stand back, ma'am. This won't be pretty! Kill the lights!!"

I have no words! Our bedroom carpet lit up like the Fourth of July.

"I've been living in this!" I said. "I've been living in a cesspool!"

"That's why I'm here, ma'am. I've been trained to handle this."

Until he shone that black light on our carpet, which made urine crystals light up, I had no idea they were there. Light has a habit of revealing what's been hidden. If you linger long enough, you'll see beyond what's immediately apparent to a much bigger story.

As a child, my son was easy to read. If he was having a good day, it was broadcast across his face in Technicolor. On a bad day I could hear emotional tornado sirens a mile away.

One afternoon, I sat in middle-school carpool, watching for the boy wearing name tag number 241 to appear. When I saw my son and the color of the storm clouds that had gathered overhead, I knew something was very wrong. He got in the back of the car, buckled up, and we drove off. I could tell he'd been crying. It was a silent ride home.

When we arrived home, I pulled into the garage and he immediately got out of the car, ran upstairs, and closed his bedroom door.

I gave him a few minutes before I went up with a mug of hot chocolate. "Do you want to talk?" I asked. He lay on his bed, seemingly grief stricken, so I put the hot chocolate on the bedside table, sat down beside him, and drew him into my arms. "Whatever's wrong, babe, let me carry it with you," I said.

The story tumbled out. He and two of his friends had stuffed enough paper towels down one of the school toilets to cause it to overflow and soak the whole bathroom floor. Not exactly smoking behind the bike shed but enough to have him sent to the principal's office. He had never been there before. The principal, after a stern lecture, told them they would be assisting the school janitor at all breaks for the next week.

"What are you most upset about?" I asked.

"Well, I'm sorry I did it, but I'm sorrier I got caught!" he said.

Reminded me of a story I heard about a man who had underpaid on his taxes, so he wrote to the IRS. "I haven't been able to sleep lately because I deliberately misrepresented my income. I am enclosing a check for $150.00, and if I still can't sleep, I'll send you the rest." That's not really guilt; it's discomfort and inconvenience.

For the next three days, Christian and his friends showed up at breaks and lunchtime to help the janitor. On the fourth day I knew something had gone wrong. Again we drove home in silence, but this time he went into the den and sat with his face in his hands, big tears leaking out between his fingers. I sat beside him, arm around his shoulders until he could talk.

"Mom, I feel so bad," he began. "The janitor is such a nice man, and what I did gave him a lot of work to do."

"Did you ask him to forgive you?" I said.

"Yes, and he forgave me. I'm just so sorry that what I did hurt him."

This time what Christian felt wasn't the inconvenience of being caught; it was the understanding that what he did impacted the life of someone else.

———— ∞ ————

King David was about to experience that same reality and light. Ultimately light would lead to healing, but first to desperate grief. David was king, a powerful king, and what he committed, he carried out mostly in secret. A couple of people knew, but they weren't going to say anything because of intimidation. Who wants to cross the king? It looked as though David had gotten away with adultery and murder. That is, unless you look at the end of the story in 2 Samuel 11 as news of Uriah's death was brought back to the king.

> So the messenger went to Jerusalem and gave a complete report to David. "The enemy came out against us in the open fields," he said. "And as we chased them back to the city gate, the archers on the wall shot arrows at us. Some of the king's men were killed, including Uriah the Hittite."
>
> "Well, tell Joab not to be discouraged," David said. "The sword devours this one today and that one tomorrow! Fight harder next time, and conquer the city!"
>
> When Uriah's wife heard that her husband was dead, she mourned for him. When the period of mourning was over, David sent for her and brought her to the palace, and she became one of his wives. Then she gave birth to a son. But the LORD was displeased with what David had done. (vv. 22–27)

How cold! Uriah was a trusted friend who willingly offered his life each day to defend his king. Now he was reduced, squeezed into the anonymous crowd of "this one and that one." "Tell Joab not to be discouraged"? Joab was sick because he knew the part he'd played in the murder of this innocent, noble man. David's sin had clouded who he was. This was not the one who had once sat under the stars, praising God for divine protection in dark and lonely places. This king was a lying man playing damage control with his life and the lives of others. But what was really going on inside his heart? Sometimes the louder we talk, the more trouble we're in.

There is an irrefutable law in the universe: "Don't be misled—you cannot mock the justice of God. You will always harvest what you plant" (Gal. 6:7).

I had a conversation with a young woman in my favorite local coffee shop one day. She asked if she could join me for a few minutes because she had a question to which no one in her family had an answer. We sat at a small circular table by the window and she began to pour out her confusion.

It had recently come to light that her pastor had been involved in an affair for more than a year. "What I don't understand," she said, "is that the last few months have been some of his best sermons. How can that be possible when he was living a lie?"

That's a hard question to answer. Only God knows the truth, but I know a couple of things. God's truth remains true no matter who delivers it or what's going on in their lives at the time. It's also possible to be called and gifted by God, to look good on the outside and shine like a new penny, but to refuse the true refining of character that comes through God's school of surrender and suffering. It's never been a popular course, but it's where true transformation happens. The first time that pastor was tempted, he should have picked himself up and run as fast as he could away from sin. I'm sure the more he gave in, the harder it was to get out. Perhaps, like David, he thought he was getting away with it. After all, his ministry seemed to be flourishing.

Paul wrote, "God's gifts and his call can never be withdrawn" (Rom. 11:29). I've heard people use this verse as a license to excuse behavior: "God called me. God gifted me. There's nothing anyone can do about that. Yada, yada, yada!"

First of all, that verse is in a passage relating to God having mercy on His chosen people, Israel. Second, what we saw clearly in the life of King Saul is that the gift might remain, but God's anointing and presence can be removed. There is a vast difference between an outward appearance of power and an inner surrender to the Holy Spirit.

Second Samuel 11 ends this way: "But the LORD was displeased with what David had done" (v. 27). One thing I'm sure of is that if you are a man or woman who loves God and wants to live a godly life, unconfessed sin tears you up inside. Did that show in David's life in the weeks and months that followed? It doesn't seem so. When we read about the confrontation David finally had with the prophet, it's natural to assume that it happened almost immediately, but notice this: it was almost a year before Nathan the prophet confronted David with his sin. We see in retrospect what was going on inside David in Psalms 32 and 51, but first came the prophetic encounter.

So the LORD sent Nathan the prophet to tell David this story: "There were two men in a certain town. One was rich, and one was poor. The rich man owned a great many sheep and cattle. The poor man owned nothing but one little lamb he had bought. He raised that little lamb, and it grew up with his children. It ate from the man's own plate and drank from his cup. He cuddled it in his arms like a baby daughter. One day a guest arrived at the home of the rich man. But instead of killing an animal from his own flock or herd, he took the poor man's lamb and killed it and prepared it for his guest."

David was furious. "As surely as the LORD lives," he vowed, "any man who would do such a thing deserves to die! He must repay four lambs to the poor man for the one he stole and for having no pity."

Then Nathan said to David, "You are that man!" (2 Sam. 12:1–7)

Imagine the scene. David loves Nathan and trusts him as a godly man. I'm sure David was glad to welcome in the prophet. Perhaps this visit would lift some of the heaviness he had been feeling inside for months. Nathan begins to tell his story as David leans in and listens. As the story unfolds, David is furious. How could anyone do such a brutal, cold-blooded thing? David passes sentence not knowing that he's passing sentence on himself, until four words turn the black-light sin detector on.

You are that man!

Just four words dispelling the darkness that David used to cover up his sin. Isn't it interesting how much easier it is to see sin in someone else's life than our own? This story has really helped me at times. Whenever I'm thinking of doing something but I have a niggling feeling that it might not be right, I use this lesson from Nathan. I imagine what I would think if someone told me that someone else had done it. This simple practice is really powerful. In some areas of my life I have a broken filter, but if I use this principle as an accurate lens for my life, I get clarity.

God's timing fascinates me. He didn't send Nathan the morning after David slept with Bathsheba or even after Uriah's death. He didn't even send him when David married her. God waited. Most theologians agree that it was about a year later.

Why would God wait? It's the mercy of God that lets us feel the impact of our sin. Until we fully understand the weight of our sin, we can't truly celebrate the beauty of our costly redemption.

Like most powerful people, King David was surrounded by those who would only tell him what he wanted to hear. That's the trouble with power. It attracts followers like moths to a flame, followers who are unwilling to confront sin or make the leader upset. Many large ministries and churches have fallen because the one "on the throne" refused the counsel of good, godly people. It might feel good for a season to have your ego stroked three times a day, but it is a far greater gift to be surrounded by those who love you enough to speak truth. Remember: "Faithful are the wounds of a friend; profuse are the kisses of an enemy" (Prov. 27:6 ESV).

Do you notice how hard David's heart has become? By Judaic law, someone who stole something from another must return it fourfold. The law gives no mention of killing the thief. David seems to be trying to clear his own conscience by punishing someone else. Like David, when we hold on to sin in our own lives, we become very judgmental of others. It's only when we have tasted grace that we can share it with another sinner. In his book on David, Alan Redpath has written, "Is that why some of us are so merciless with the Christian who is tripped up? Is that why we have no gospel for the believer who falls? It may be not because we are very holy, but because we are so unholy, that we condemn the thing in another as we refuse to judge it in our own lives."[2]

Or to put it more bluntly, consider what Jesus said about the woman caught in adultery: "Let him who is without sin among you be the first to throw a stone at her" (John 8:7 ESV).

Nathan wasn't finished with David. He was there on a divine mission delivering every word God would speak to David:

> "Thus says the LORD, the God of Israel, 'I anointed you king over Israel, and I delivered you out of the hand of Saul. And I gave you your master's house and your master's wives into your arms and gave you the house of Israel and of Judah. And if this were too little, I would add to you as much more. Why have you despised the word of the LORD, to do what is evil in his sight? You have struck down Uriah the Hittite with the sword and have taken his wife to be your wife and have killed him with the sword of the Ammonites. Now therefore the sword shall never depart

from your house, because you have despised me and have taken the wife of Uriah the Hittite to be your wife.' Thus says the LORD, 'Behold, I will raise up evil against you out of your own house. And I will take your wives before your eyes and give them to your neighbor, and he shall lie with your wives in the sight of this sun. For you did it secretly, but I will do this thing before all Israel and before the sun.'" (2 Sam. 12:7–12 ESV)

What a harsh word that must've been to hear. Terrifying too. Nathan reminded David of the lavish kindness and faithfulness of God to him. Then he moved to the drastic consequences of his sin: "the sword shall never depart from your house."

As I've read David's story over and over, I've wondered, did God wait for almost a year to give David an opportunity to confess his sin without Nathan's message? Would the consequences have been less had David chosen to humble himself before God alone? Only God knows the answer to that question. What we do know is how David responded to this prophetic word. "David said to Nathan, 'I have sinned against the LORD'" (2 Sam. 12:13 ESV).

That's it! That's his whole response.

There's no, "I know it was wrong, but I was really tired, and I don't think she should have been out on the roof, bathing, anyway. She must have known I would have seen her!" He didn't say, "I ordered Uriah to go sleep with his wife. If he'd done that, none of this would have happened!" All he said was, "I have sinned against the LORD." He didn't even say, "I've sinned against Uriah" or Bathsheba or Joab or any of his own wives. David understood that the one he had greatly sinned against was the Lord. Had he wronged others? Absolutely. But God felt the weight of his sin most acutely.

Contrast that with Saul's response when the prophet Samuel confronted him with the fact that he could hear the bleating of sheep and lowing of oxen after being told to slaughter every one. "'It's true that the army spared the best of the sheep, goats, and cattle,' Saul admitted. 'But they are going to sacrifice them to the LORD your God. We have destroyed everything else'" (1 Sam. 15:15). Saul tried to justify what he'd allowed and attempted to spiritualize his disobedience. Samuel responded, "What is more pleasing to the LORD: your burnt offerings and sacrifices or your obedience to his voice?" (v. 22). We learn here that God is not interested in religious excuses or blame shifting. Blame is simply another way of diffusing our anger or pain onto someone else. God is solely interested in our hearts and their responsiveness to His voice.

Finally, David's heart's response was to own what he had done. There's such grace here for you and me. If you look at Saul's sin and David's sin with twenty-first-century eyes, David's looks so much more acute. Adultery and murder would trump disobedience to a few commands any day in our book. We can't weigh, though, the significance of what Saul did. He touched things that were holy to God and repeatedly did his own thing, living firmly outside the will and voice of God in defiance. No matter how deeply we understand the implication of these things, the hope tucked into both sordid tales is that when we own our sin, God forgives us.

Grace is amazing, as the song goes, but it doesn't erase the effects of our deliberate sin. There were serious consequences for David's sin. The baby born to David and Bathsheba died. Yet even after the tears of that loss dried, redemption bloomed with the birth of Solomon. David's son would ultimately become the king's successor, the builder of the stunning temple, and the wisest king to ever rule. Solomon wrote this: "People who conceal their sins will not prosper, but if they confess and turn from them, they will receive mercy" (Prov. 28:13). Where do you think Solomon absorbed that lesson? Don't you think it's likely that he learned it from his father? That's the other great gift that comes out of the night of poor choices: we have real hope and wisdom to offer to those who come after us.

Your life is a story that will be read by others. We can choose to conceal the parts we consider failures and pump up the good stuff, or we can live as an open book, grateful for where redemption found us but did not leave us. If you've made poor choices in your life, I urge you not to hide. Instead allow the piercing light of God's love to reveal the sin and heal your heart in the aftermath.

I don't mean that you should indiscriminately begin to pour out your story to those who may not be in a place to receive it. Christ warned that we should not cast our pearls before swine (see Matt. 7:6 KJV). In other words, don't take what's holy to you and give it to those who will only trample on it. Be wise in your disclosure. But when you have received a degree of deep healing, pay attention to those to whom the Holy Spirit directs you so that you can share the hope that now lives in you. Our story is one of the greatest gifts we can give each other. Paul wrote, "All praise to God, the Father of our Lord Jesus Christ. God is our merciful Father and the source of all comfort. He comforts us in all our troubles so that we can comfort others. When they are troubled, we will be able to give them the same comfort God has given us" (2 Cor. 1:3–4).

Our scars can give life to others so that their scars might be smaller. Your wounds might even turn another life around.

Alfred Nobel was born in Sweden in 1866. You probably don't know much about the man but may well be familiar with his legacy as the creator of the Nobel Peace Prize. Alfred was fascinated by physics and chemistry. He spent time studying in Paris with a young Italian chemist, Ascanio Sobrero, who had invented nitroglycerine. After Alfred moved back to Sweden, he continued experimenting with this highly combustible substance, but his experiments went terribly wrong, resulting in the death of his younger brother, Emil. Even so, he persevered. He discovered that if you mix nitroglycerine with a type of fine sand called kieselguhr, it could be made into a paste that could be shaped into rods. He called his discovery *dynamite*.

When he died, his last will and testament stated that his wealth should be given as prizes to those who had done their best for humanity in physics, chemistry, and literature, and to those who pursue peace. His family contested it for four years, but finally the first Nobel Prize was granted in 1901. Someone who made his fortune developing a substance that can be used to cause great destruction left that wealth to those who fight for beauty, healing, and peace. A flower bloomed from a place of great loss and sorrow.

So, too, with David.

Even as Nathan turned to leave, did David pick up his pen and write these words?

> *Have mercy on me, O God,*
>> *because of your unfailing love.*
> *Because of your great compassion,*
>> *blot out the stain of my sins.*
> *Wash me clean from my guilt.*
>> *Purify me from my sin.*
> *For I recognize my rebellion;*
>> *it haunts me day and night.*
> *Against you, and you alone, have I sinned;*
>> *I have done what is evil in your sight.*
> *You will be proved right in what you say,*
>> *and your judgment against me is just.*
> *For I was born a sinner—*
>> *yes, from the moment my mother conceived me.*
> *But you desire honesty from the womb,*
>> *teaching me wisdom even there.*

Purify me from my sins, and I will be clean;
    wash me, and I will be whiter than snow.
Oh, give me back my joy again;
    you have broken me—
    now let me rejoice.
Don't keep looking at my sins.
    Remove the stain of my guilt.
Create in me a clean heart, O God.
    Renew a loyal spirit within me.
Do not banish me from your presence,
    and don't take your Holy Spirit from me.

Restore to me the joy of your salvation
    and make me willing to obey you.
                    (Ps. 51:1–12)

King David had been trapped in absolute misery for a year. It may have looked to others as if life were moving along as normal, but in Psalm 32 he penned poignant words about what happens to us when we try to bury our sin and move on with life in the shadows.

When I refused to confess my sin,
    my body wasted away,
    and I groaned all day long.
Day and night your hand of discipline was heavy on me.
    My strength evaporated like water in the summer heat. Interlude

Finally, I confessed all my sins to you
    and stopped trying to hide my guilt.
I said to myself, "I will confess my rebellion to the LORD."
    And you forgave me! All my guilt is gone. Interlude
                    (vv. 3–5)

"All my guilt is gone"! What a powerful statement. You can spend your whole life longing to go back and change a moment or a decision, but you can't change the past. What God offers you is grace and forgiveness in the present and hope for the future.

I saw that grace clearly in the eyes of a pastor's wife who asked to speak to me after an event in the Midwest. She'd had an abortion in college and never told anyone, not even her parents. "I couldn't have a baby; I just wanted to get on with my life," she said. After she got married they tried for some time to get pregnant and couldn't. "I knew it was my fault. I knew God was angry with me and punishing me." Her grief was so intense she became ill. Believing that she was dying, she told her husband the secret that had wrapped around her soul like a millstone. "He forgave me," she said. "He told me he loved me and that God loved me too." With this weight cast into the sea, she began to get well, stronger every day.

I remember her saying, "When you told your story about your depression and how ashamed you felt at first but how God is using it to help others, I told God that I'd do the same. I don't want any other woman to suffer alone. I wanted to make my past all right. I can't do that, but God made me right with Him. I think that's better, don't you?"

I do! God is so much bigger than your past. He is so much more merciful than your sin. He is so much stronger than your weakest moment. His plans for you are so much greater than your failures. He is for you. Always for you! God's grace is like the penetrating black light of the carpet cleaner who salvaged our bedroom carpet. The mess was exposed but not left that way. So, too, God restores us so that we can walk from that renewed place and share our story with others who are broken, one woman at a time. It's a message this world, yes, even the church, is longing to hear. You can be clean. You can be set free!

EIGHT

The Longing for What Would Glorify God

David walked up the road to the Mount of Olives,
weeping as he went. His head was covered and
his feet were bare as a sign of mourning. And
the people who were with him covered their
heads and wept as they climbed the hill.
—*2 Samuel 15:30*

It was a long and gloomy night that gathered
on me, haunted by the ghosts of many hopes,
of many dear remembrances, many errors,
many unavailing sorrows and regrets.[1]
—*Charles Dickens, David Copperfield*

ONLY FIFTEEN PEOPLE WERE IN THE COURTROOM
that morning in 2015. Barry and I sat on the third bench from the front
on the left. It looked like a scene from the television show *The People's
Court*. We were a few minutes early, so I looked to see if our lawyer was
already here. I saw her long, blond hair before I saw her face. She was
talking to the court clerk. When she finished submitting paperwork, she
sat beside us. "How are you guys doing?" she asked.

"We're good," Barry said.

I looked around. Two men sat in the back row behind us with a stack of paperwork, looking as if they had slept in their suits. A man sat alone on the back row on the right. He seemed nervous and kept rubbing a tissue between his fingers until it looked as if it had snowed on his pants.

"Are we first up?" I asked.

"No, number four."

"Do we say anything at this hearing?" I asked.

"Not unless the judge calls for you."

It's a very particular sound a judge's gavel makes. Two sharp cracks of hardwood onto a sound block, demanding respect and attention. We were all on our feet before I could yell out, "Guilty!" I suddenly had this bizarre desire to laugh, so I bit the inside of my cheek until it bled. The judge took her seat, and we all sat down.

Scenes from the Woody Allen movie *Bananas* played over and over in my head. Did you ever see that one? Woody Allen plays the character Fielding Mellish, who, in a desperate attempt to impress an activist girl-friend, gets involved in a revolution in San Marcos and ends up as their president. My favorite part of the movie is where he is defending himself in court. The judge comes in, bangs the gavel twice, and Fielding immediately launches into a tirade. "I object, your honor. This trial is a travesty. It's a travesty of a mockery of a sham of two mockeries of a travesty . . ." It goes on!

On this day in court, I hadn't eaten any breakfast. I felt lightheaded at the surreal scene before me. I thought at any moment one of my friends would walk in and say, "Just kidding. We gotcha!"

Suddenly I heard the judge call out our case number. Our lawyer took her place. In that moment everything changed. Nothing was funny any-more. I had a tight knot in my stomach. I thought I might throw up. I'd been told that this judge was tough, and she was in true form that morning. We took hours to prepare all the paperwork required for bankruptcy court, but she tore it to shreds. We'd carefully filled it in as we'd been instructed, but she changed all the rules that morning and told us to come back in a month. She dismissed us. When we got outside, our lawyer fumed.

"Why did she do that?" I asked.

"Because she can!" she said.

"What did we do wrong?"

"Nothing," she said, wiping her forehead with the sleeve of her jacket. "She has the power. And if she feels like it, she can change the rules. Let's take a couple of days and touch base. We'll start again."

It was raining, so Barry went to get the car. I was in my "court clothes." Suit, hose, pumps with a medium heel. I kicked them off and sat on the edge of a large planter.

"Lord, how did we get here?"

December 3, 1994

Smiling, I woke up before the alarm went off. I looked out of the hotel window in downtown Charleston as it started to snow. Perfect!

My wedding day.

I had never intended to remarry. After five years as cohost of *The 700 Club,* I'd moved to Southern California to attend Fuller Seminary. I longed to get back to my roots, my foundation in Christ. I had no clear idea of what I would do next, but it was my desire to bury my heart in the Word of God. Being in a master's program was quite different from undergraduate work. Most of my classmates had been in ministry for some time and were taking time out to further prepare for the work God had called them to. It cost them time and money, so they were serious in their pursuit. I loved every moment. After a C. S. Lewis class or a lecture on church history, we'd sit on the benches outside the cafeteria and talk about what we were learning. I was so grateful.

Life then was simple and good.

Steve Arterburn, a longtime friend, called me one day and asked if I'd have lunch with Barry, a television producer. Steve and I had talked about the possibility of having a talk show someday. We wanted a format where Christians who had experienced brokenness could talk about real issues and the faithfulness of God when life seems over. I told him I'd be glad to meet Barry, but anything like that would be much farther down the road for me. I was learning to talk less and listen more. One of the gifts of what Saint John of the Cross deemed the "dark night" (of the soul) is that your vision changes; you see people differently. I wanted time to let everything new take root.

I liken this time in my life to the story in Mark's gospel:

When they arrived at Bethsaida, some people brought a blind man to Jesus, and they begged him to touch the man and heal him. Jesus took the blind man by the hand and led him out of the village. Then, spitting on the man's eyes, he laid his hands on him and asked, "Can you see anything now?"

The man looked around. "Yes," he said, "I see people, but I can't see them very clearly. They look like trees walking around."

Then Jesus placed his hands on the man's eyes again, and his eyes were opened. His sight was completely restored, and he could see everything clearly. (Mark 8:22–25)

For the first thirty-something years of my life, I was like that man who saw people as shapes, trees. I listened, but not as much to really understand what the other person was saying as to *fix* him or her. I was sure that whatever was wrong with someone, I had a verse for it. Yes, I was a party-on-wheels then!

But God's school of suffering changed me. I learned about what I call the companionship of brokenness—those who love God, but don't have all the pat answers.

I agreed to meet Barry at the studio where he produced a show. I was immediately struck by his looks. He had blond hair, a lot of it, and blue eyes. We only talked for about thirty minutes that night, but I couldn't get him out of my head. We met again a couple of weeks later for lunch, then again for dinner that turned into dinner and a movie. These meetings started to overwhelm me. I really liked him, but I didn't want to. I decided I had to tell him.

"I really like you, Barry," I said. "I think you're fun to be with, but you need to know that I'm divorced. It's not even been two years yet. Also I have a broken 'picker,' so I don't trust my heart. I don't think I can see you anymore. I'm really sorry."

He said he understood and we went our separate ways—for a few weeks. But I missed him, so I asked my best friends, Frank and Marlene, if they would have dinner with the two of us. I wanted to get their gut reaction.

They liked him a lot.

Part of me longed to love and be loved, but a louder part of me was terrified. All I wanted to do for the rest of my life was live in a way that would bring glory to God. What if I made another mistake?

That's the hard part of life, isn't it? If past longings have taken us down a destructive path, how do we trust our gut again?

We left David deeply repentant for his affair with Bathsheba and the murder of her husband, Uriah. Yet even in judgment, God showed mercy. A man who sleeps with another man's wife should be stoned according to Mosaic law. When you add complicity to murder, there would be no reprieve.

"Then David confessed to Nathan, 'I have sinned against the Lord.' Nathan replied, 'Yes, but the Lord has forgiven you, and you won't die for this sin'" (2 Sam. 12:13).

The long-term consequences, however, were devastating. The child Bathsheba carried only lived seven days. Not only that, but God would hold David accountable not just as king, but also as a father. The seeds he had deliberately sown would bear disastrous fruit in his home. "Because of what you have done, I will cause your own household to rebel against you. I will give your wives to another man before your very eyes, and he will go to bed with them in public view. You did it secretly, but I will make this happen to you openly in the sight of all Israel" (vv. 11–12).

What a sentence! I am sure that for the rest of his life David regretted that one-night stand with another man's wife. As John Lawrence wrote, "Confession and forgiveness in no way stop the harvest."[2]

Now, before you decide that this chapter is too depressing, let me explain what I'd like to do here. Two things:

1. We'll look at the consequences of bad choices. We can learn from the mistakes of others so that we are not easily tempted to repeat them.
2. We'll look at the questions: "What do you do in times like these? How do you live when things can't be quickly fixed?" In other words, how do you live in a way that glorifies God in a hard place?

Are you still with me?

Good, because the bottom line is, no matter how many bad choices or mistakes we make or others have made, God continues to be faithful!

Let's take a look at the severe consequences of David's choices. They are also the type of judgment that we associate with the Old Testament. It's tempting to camp out in the grace of the New Testament and think that because of Christ's sacrifice, we no longer face the consequences of our sin. That is simply not true according to the apostle Paul. "Don't be misled—you cannot mock the justice of God. You will always harvest what you plant" (Gal. 6:7). Christ's sacrifice provides forgiveness and restoration of peace with God, but as you know, certain decisions carry consequences with them.

* An affair may lead to the end of a marriage.
* Embezzling from a company may end up in jail time.
* A teen caught drinking may get expelled from school.

For every confessed sin there is forgiveness. Still, some consequences have to be walked through.

You can read the whole story of the significant events that impacted David and his family in 2 Samuel 12–24, but I'll outline them briefly in this chapter. Understanding the depth of David's pain will help us grasp the redemptive grace of God that would still pour out upon his life.

The first tragedy was the loss of the child Bathsheba carried. One commentator I read said the pain of that was removed when she gave birth to Solomon. Only someone who has lost a child knows that's not true. Of course David and Bathsheba (now married) loved this new baby, but nothing salves the pain of a lost child.

When Christian was two, I got pregnant again. We were so excited that he would have a sibling. Barry was longing for a girl and I just wanted a healthy baby, but we lost that little one at about twelve weeks. Because of that loss, there is a permanently empty room in my heart.

The next event in David's family is particularly troubling. Two of his children, Absalom and Tamar, had the same mother. Amnon was also David's son but had a different mother. Amnon lusted after his half sister. We read in 2 Samuel 13 how Amnon tricked Tamar into believing he was ill, and once she was in his room, he raped her. By this violation, Tamar's life was essentially over. She was disgraced. She ran to the one she trusted most, her brother Absalom.

For two years Absalom did nothing. He didn't address the sin or even speak to his brother. He just waited for his moment to avenge his sister.

I'm tempted to wonder where David was during all of this? If you have two sons who don't speak a word to each other for two years, I think you would notice. Hopefully you'd try to mediate. I wonder if David didn't want to have his own mess thrown back in his face. But making poor choices at one point in life doesn't mean we abdicate our responsibility as parents. Our mistakes can be our shame or our story. We can grab hold of what the enemy meant for evil and say, "Yes, that's true, but by God's grace I am a different woman," or a different man. It would seem that David did nothing.

Two years later Absalom threw a feast during sheep-shearing time, intending to set a trap. He invited all the king's sons, but asked David specifically to send Amnon. David was initially reluctant, but Absalom begged and pleaded until David finally said yes.

It's hard sometimes holding the line with our kids. We say no, but they don't quit, and sometimes it's just easier to say yes to stop the begging.

Well, David would regret giving in. Amnon was the eldest son, by rights the crown prince next in line to the throne. He wouldn't live to see morning. Absalom told his men to wait until Amnon was drunk and then kill him.

When David's other sons saw their brother's blood pooling on the ground, they ran away. Absalom escaped to his grandfather and stayed there for three years.

So we have the death of a child, the rape of his daughter by her half brother, and the murder of that son by his brother. The seeds of rebellion had been planted deep because an even greater crop would grow. A brother avenging the rape of his sister is something I think any of us can understand, but Absalom had a lust for power and control. He determined to overthrow his father and make himself king. You can read that full story in 2 Samuel 15. Absalom ran his own political campaign, beguiling the people. Power and charisma can be an intoxicating mix, but without character, it's a recipe for disaster.

Absalom wooed the affection of the people of Israel away from his father. When David heard about the rebellious uprising, he knew that they were coming after him. Once more he had to run for his life from the palace. We read that "the king and all his people set out on foot, pausing at the last house" (2 Sam. 15:17). What must that have been like for David to look back on Jerusalem, that great city named after him, the City of David, not knowing if he would ever return?

"David walked up the road to the Mount of Olives, weeping as he went. His head was covered and his feet were bare as a sign of mourning" (v. 30).

Covered head, feet bare: a familiar sign, a sign anyone could read. King David was bankrupt.

2006

"I love the house," I said, "but we haven't sold our other one yet."

"My worry is that if we don't get it now, it'll be gone," Barry answered.

We'd been living in the Dallas, Texas, area for four years. Our son, Christian, was eight. When we chose our house, we didn't pay enough attention to the fact that it was right by a high school and teenage drivers raced through the streets, giving little thought to an eight-year-old on his bike. It really worried me, so we decided to sell and find a quieter neighborhood. We found the house we wanted. But would ours sell in time?

Finally a couple put down an offer we accepted. The only issue was that we'd have to close on the new one before completing the deal on the old. Still, it all seemed good. The family buying our house had older children who would be going to the high school, so it seemed perfect. A done deal.

Interesting word, *seemed*. Ever been held hostage by "seemed"?

* It seemed like the right decision at the time.
* She seemed like the perfect person for the job.
* She seemed like the perfect babysitter.
* He seemed like a good guy.

I'm sure you saw this coming, but before the ink dried on our new contract, the buyers for our old house dropped out, as did the entire housing market in Dallas that year. For five years we carried two mortgages. Not just an extra mortgage, but also the upkeep of our old home. I learned during the next couple of years that the sin of omission could be as devastating as the sin of commission.

Barry is a perfectionist. He loves style and design and really went to town on our new home. I'd come back from speaking dates and the carpet was different or the light fixtures had been changed. When I asked why they were different, he'd just say something about trading out with the builder. I never pushed it further. The reality was he had spent a small fortune on this "perfect" home that would become our debtors prison. I worked as hard as I could for the next few years to try to pay the debt down, but in the fall of 2014, we had to face it: we were in over our heads.

I was so ashamed. I was angry too. We'd made an agreement before we married that we'd never spend more than we had. We failed miserably. Everything we own belongs to the Lord, but we had spent it as if it were ours to squander. I thought of all the moms and children I'd met in Africa, the Philippines, and the Dominican Republic who have so little, but live with deep gratitude. I thought of my own upbringing, when my mum had so little after my dad's death but never went a penny into debt. The weight of what we had done crushed me.

At our first meeting with the bankruptcy attorney, Barry answered most of her questions while I nursed a cup of coffee until it was cold. She asked, "Are you trying to get rid of some of your debt?"

He said, "No. We want to pay back every penny, but we just didn't know how to do it."

And so the debt-repayment process began. Month after month of reports of every single penny we made, credit cards gone, and one checking account with the name *Debtor in possession* printed like an accusation on every check. (I considered changing my name to Sheila Debtor-in-Possession, but it seemed clumsy.)

Our efforts all led up to that morning in court when we presented our plan to pay back everything we owed. It should have been pretty straightforward. We weren't trying to wiggle out of anything. Our attorney had presented countless cases laid out just like ours to this judge. But on that particular morning, she didn't like the way our paperwork looked. So we thanked her and vacated the courtroom.

My question, the passionate cry of my heart as I sat on the edge of the planter, was this, "How can we possibly bring glory to Your name out of this mess, Lord?"

Consequences.

We can't escape them.

Perhaps you are there now.

Forgiveness is a beautiful, costly gift offered when we've messed up, but grace is what we need for the long walk home toward wholeness. Some situations can be resolved in a moment. Others take a long time. Even our very salvation must be worked out, as Paul wrote to the church in Philippi: "Therefore, my dear friends, as you have always obeyed—not only in my presence, but now much more in my absence—continue to work out your salvation with fear and trembling, for it is God who works in you to will and to act in order to fulfill his good purpose" (Phil. 2:12–13 NIV).

I'd volunteered to speak in a women's prison the night before I would speak at a conference in the same town. I went in early and was allowed to spend the better part of the day meeting with various women enrolled in the faith-based part of the prison. It was amazing to see the curriculum that the ministry offered: Bible teaching, parenting skills, housekeeping, and all sorts of practical lessons that would hopefully serve these women well on the outside. Their stories were heartbreaking.

Some struggled with drug addiction and had taken to prostitution to support their habit or the habit of a boyfriend. Many had young children on the outside and showed me pictures of bright little faces that should have been wrapped up in their mothers' arms. One girl in particular looked so out of place. She looked like a doll: thin, with blond hair and pale cheeks. She had the sweetest smile. Her story is not mine to tell, but the horrors that this child faced were unspeakable.

One day, when she couldn't take it anymore, she picked up a knife and fought back. Now she was locked away for protecting herself when no one else would. I think she must have seen into my soul as I privately raged to God about the injustice of this girl's life because she put her hand on my arm. I'm paraphrasing her response: "Sheila, this is the best thing that ever happened to me. Behind these walls I found a relationship with a God who died for me. I'll never be alone again."

As I led worship that night with three hundred female prisoners, I saw her, arms raised to heaven, grateful to our God, who makes beauty out of ashes. This precious young woman showed me how to bring glory to God in a hard, hard place.

But what about our great hymn writer?

We left the psalmist grieving and weeping as he walked up the road to the Mount of Olives. Only God knows the reason for all those tears.

Tears of regret.

Tears of betrayal.

Tears of loss.

But what we do have is what he wrote during that time. David wrote Psalm 3 when he fled from Absalom. It gives us a glimpse into his heart.

> O Lord, I have so many enemies;
>> so many are against me.
> So many are saying,
>> "God will never rescue him!"
>
> But you, O Lord, are a shield around me;
>> you are my glory, the one who holds my head high.
> I cried out to the Lord,
>> and he answered me from his holy mountain.
>
> I lay down and slept,
>> yet I woke up in safety,
>> for the Lord was watching over me.
> I am not afraid of ten thousand enemies
>> who surround me on every side.
>> (vv. 1–6)

Here King David, living with the consequences of his sin, models how to live. We worship! When nothing else makes sense, we thank God for who He is and how He loves us. We cry out to the heavens and declare to our wounded hearts that the Lord watches over us. He is our shield! He is our defender! He is the one who holds our heads up high when we want to bury them in a pillow.

If you are in a tough place right now, write out this prayer of David. Pray it over yourself. As you look in the mirror, pray it out loud. When someone tells you that you'll never get out of this mess, find a quiet place and declare this truth over and over until it's louder than the enemy's lies. The truth is that no matter how things appear and no matter what we feel, God is in control.

Now I want us to think about one more thing.

David could have fought Absalom. He was a powerful, charismatic king, a great warrior. So don't you think that David, instead of running from Jerusalem, could have rallied all of Israel again to come against his rebellious son?

Here we find a profound lesson on what it looks like to be a person after God's own heart. Under the rabid rule of King Saul, David never fought to be king, even though he was the anointed one. Now, as king he refused to fight to keep the crown. Saul fought, lied, and disobeyed to keep control of his power. In that manic struggle, he lost not only his power but also his mind and, most devastating of all, the presence of the Lord.

David refused to fight for power. His bottom line was, "If God is through with me, then I am through. If He's not, then no matter what anyone tries to do, God will vindicate me." What a powerful place of rest and peace. More than God's power, David desired His will. I love the way Gene Edwards pictures David as he willingly walks away from the palace and the kingdom, "The true king turned and walked quietly out of the throne room, out of the palace, out of the city. He walked and he walked . . . into the bosoms of all men (and women) whose hearts are pure."[3]

God was about to restore David to the throne. No one could have imagined that it would be the very thing that Absalom was praised for that would lead to his downfall.

"Now Absalom was praised as the most handsome man in all Israel. He was flawless from head to foot. He cut his hair only once a year, and then only because it was so heavy. When he weighed it out, it came to five pounds" (2 Sam. 14:25–26).

I can't imagine what he must have looked like . . . flawless from head to foot. What he saw in the reflecting pool each morning told him he was invincible. If only he could have stayed a little longer and looked a little deeper behind his perfect eyes to his troubled, rebellious soul. He was another Saul in the making. Those who grab power and are willing to do anything to hold on to it will never trust those around them. They will see in others what they refuse to own in themselves. Absalom's final insult to his father was a sad fulfillment of the final piece of Nathan's prophecy to David, "I will give your wives to another man before your very eyes, and he will go to bed with them in public view."

Having ousted his father from the throne and the palace, Absalom committed the final act of degrading his father's honor: "They set up a tent on the palace roof where everyone could see it, and Absalom went in and had sex with his father's concubines" (2 Sam. 16:22). He did this in public, where everyone could see, in the same place where David had lusted after Bathsheba.

I wonder if for a moment he stopped and thought about his father's God? No matter who sat on the throne in that exquisite palace, there exists One who sits on the throne forever. This King will not be mocked.

That same day was a battle day. Absalom and his men would pursue David to kill him. Perhaps Absalom was so filled with hate that his vision clouded, because he would not survive that day.

> During the battle, Absalom happened to come upon some of David's men. He tried to escape on his mule, but as he rode beneath the thick branches of a great tree, his hair got caught in the tree. . . . Then [Joab] took three daggers and plunged them into Absalom's heart as he dangled, still alive, in the great tree. Ten of Joab's young armor bearers then surrounded Absalom and killed him. (2 Sam. 18:9, 14–15)

There is great irony in Absalom's death. Caught and hung by the very thing he took such pride in. David's men finished him off and buried him beneath a pile of stones.

So girls, how do we live through the tough times? What do we do when the road ahead is a long one? How do we bring glory to God in a tough place?

We worship even when there's no light on the path or dawn on the horizon.

Why?

Because God is worth our deepest devotion, and He is faithful.

Let's join our brother David and say with him, "I lay down and slept, yet I woke up in safety, for the Lord was watching over me."

Amen, David!

As I write, there is a long road ahead of walking through this bankruptcy. It's not a journey I ever wanted to take. It's certainly not something I'm proud of, so why did I share it? We're all going through something. I want you to know that you are not alone. The enemy would love to isolate us and make us believe that life is working just perfectly for everyone but us. That's not true. Perhaps you're in a place like that right now. It might be a health issue or concern for a loved one or any one of life's myriad challenges. So how do we stand in the days we never dreamed would happen? Each day I begin with this one verse:

> Let the morning bring me word of your unfailing love,
>   for I have put my trust in you.
> Show me the way I should go,
>   for to you I entrust my life.
> (Ps. 143:8 NIV)

I love this verse because David is saying, "Let the morning bring me word of *God's* unfailing love, not mine." You and I will fail, but God will never fail us. Don't wait for the storm to be over before you begin to worship.

NINE

The Longing to Share the Grace and Mercy We've Received from God

All praise to God, the Father of our Lord Jesus Christ.
God is our merciful Father and the source of all
comfort. He comforts us in all our troubles so that we
can comfort others. When they are troubled, we will be
able to give them the same comfort God has given us.
—*2 Corinthians 1:3–4*

Suffering, failure, loneliness, sorrow, discouragement,
and death will be part of your journey, but
the Kingdom of God will conquer all these
horrors. No evil can resist grace forever.[1]
—*Brennan Manning*

"LET'S TAKE SEPARATE CARS," I SUGGESTED TO
Barry. "I'll meet you there. Then you'll be able to go straight back to the office."

It was the winter of 2015, we were meeting with a marriage counselor, and I was bone weary. The weight of his out-of-control spending in the past was something I carried every day. Some days I felt hopeful that we could climb this seemingly insurmountable hill, and on other days I was resentful that I had to.

"I could come home and we could go together," he countered.

"No, let's take separate cars. We might be upset with each other," I shot back.

"Are you anticipating being upset?" he asked. I heard the hitch in his voice.

"I might be." I hung up.

Summer 1994

We sat in our marriage counselor's office, grinning like two Cheshire cats.

"Have you set a date for the wedding?" the counselor asked.

"Yes, December 3," Barry answered.

"So no sleeveless dress for you, I guess," he said with a smile.

"I'm not much of a sleeveless person," I responded. "My upper arms wiggle."

"No, they don't!" Barry said through the Coke-bottle lens of love.

"So tell me," the counselor continued, "what are the things that are most important to each of you in a partner?"

I'm ashamed to admit this, but I don't remember anything Barry said. I do remember mine—funny, that!

"Only two things really matter to me," I said. "Everything else is negotiable. One, it's really important that we stay intimate and connected. And two, that we never spend more than we have, and we tithe way more than 10 percent."

"Sounds reasonable," he said. "What do you think, Barry?"

"Great! What's way more?" Barry asked.

"I'd like us ultimately to be able to tithe 40 percent of our income."

"Wow, that's a lot, but sure!" Barry grabbed my hand. His eyes made the promise.

We started off really well. We connected on a deep level and our love grew sweeter each year. Sure, we had our fights and issues, but life was good. The money? Well, all seemed to be going well. I took care of paying all the bills, as Barry isn't much of a detail person.

That shifted one day over lunch with a friend who is also a counselor. I don't remember how the conversation shifted to finances, but he asked who took care of the money in our home. We said that I did. He asked Barry how he felt about that, and Barry confessed that it made him feel a little emasculated.

"Do you want to take over our finances?" I asked.

"I'd love to," he said.

I'm not sure when things began to go wrong.

Bad choices begin slowly. Infidelity, alcoholism, overspending, workaholism, or any number of evils that can corrode the lining of the best relationship usually start in small, manageable ways. We notice it, but it's easy to explain away.

* "My husband never listens to me anymore, so it's good to have someone to talk to at work."
* "I just need one drink, to relax."
* "If we just had this one more thing, the house would be perfect."
* "I get more work done at the office after everyone else has gone home."

I don't think anyone wakes up one morning and thinks, *This would be the perfect day to endanger my marriage!* But unchecked, even the smallest slip can cause an avalanche.

In the early years it began with wanting the perfect car, then the perfect home. Then when that home proved to be less than perfect, we moved again. Then we needed a bigger home with more furniture.

We had a horrible confrontation on my fiftieth birthday. My sister Frances and my mum, Betty, were visiting from Scotland to celebrate with us, and Barry asked them to take me out for brunch so he could get my surprise ready. I had no idea what it could be.

A few weeks before, Barry had been flipping through a magazine and showed me a picture of a hand-painted Italian bed. He asked me if I liked it. I told him that I thought it was lovely, but we had a beautiful new bed, so I didn't want another one. But on this day, when we got back to the house, Barry asked me to close my eyes. He led me into our bedroom. I opened my eyes to see the new Italian bed, two new side tables, and a hand-painted Italian chest. I burst into tears.

"What's wrong?" he said. "This is your birthday gift!"

"Barry, this is for you. It's not for me!" I yelled.

It wasn't a good birthday.

Some of the hardest questions I've had to ask myself, as I finally began to understand the amount of debt we were in, were, "Where was I when all this happened?" and "Why didn't I do something or say something?" It's much easier for me to attribute blame than to hold myself accountable for the role I played or refused to play. Yes, Barry had taken out loans and spent a lot of money on things we didn't need, but I'd signed the papers. I was there when things were delivered. Sometimes I would speak up, but never in a way that helped. I'd let things build up inside me, wait until I was really mad, then let him have it.

I've asked myself many times why I lived like this for so long in our marriage. Part of it is that I hated when we had confrontations. Barry would get very defensive and underplay what he'd spent. When he felt attacked, he would withdraw, and I felt alone. It took us years to learn the art of sitting down like two mature adults and face real issues together.

Barry is a perfectionist. It's a punishing way to live because we are all fatally flawed. He's very designer-label conscious, so I decided to see if I could fool him one birthday. Fat chance! I bought a jacket at Goodwill and had it dry-cleaned. Then I gently removed a label from one of his expensive jackets and carefully attached it. He opened the box, felt the fabric, and said, "You're fooling no one!" Dang!

I don't know if you're a fan of the television sitcom *Everybody Loves Raymond*. We love it and have watched every single episode enough times to have the scripts memorized! One of the things that made no sense to me at first was that Marie (the mother) still had the plastic covering on the sofa they bought years ago. The longer we were married, the more I began to realize that Marie's sofa would be Barry's happy place! We still have two chairs that none of us have sat on. Apparently we're waiting for the Queen to visit.

Every now and again I try to help him loosen up. Don't you know he just loves that?! A few years ago I leased a new car. There is something so lovely about that new-car smell and shiny interior. But I knew that for at least the first year, Barry would want me to park about half a mile away from the nearest vehicle. So, on the day I drove it home, I asked him to come outside. I grabbed a small stone and threw it at the driver's side door, making a little ding. I'm sure my mum heard Barry's wails of shock clear in Scotland.

"There!" I said. "It's not perfect anymore. Now I can park like a regular person."

It wasn't very kind but it worked.

Part of Barry's brokenness is that his parents loved him, but really smothered him. They waited eleven years before being able to get pregnant, and once he arrived, they determined nothing bad would ever happen to him. He was never allowed to do a sleepover at a friend's house or play sports or anything that appeared innately risky. Instead, they bought him things, a lot of things. So "things" represented love to Barry.

Part of my brokenness is that I expect to get hurt. God in His great grace and mercy has healed me of so much, but tucked away somewhere there is still a little of the five-year-old girl waiting to be betrayed and abandoned. That also means when I do feel betrayed, I bring a boatload of baggage with me. It's not fair, but it's true.

As I drove to meet Barry at our counselor's office, I resisted the temptation to turn on the radio and drown out my thoughts. Instead I talked to my Father.

I don't know what to do here, I prayed silently. *It's not as if he made a small bad choice, or a one-off. His decisions will affect us for years. I only asked for two things, just two things, but this financial mess had clouded both. I'm trying not to be angry, but I am angry. Who needs five sofas? Who in their right mind has a chandelier over the bathtub? The electrician made me sign a paper that says if it falls in and I get electrocuted, my family won't sue him! I'm ashamed, Lord. You've given us so much, and we've messed up big-time. If he doesn't change, then when Christian goes off to college in the fall, I'm going to live in a little apartment by myself! We'll still be married and he can come and visit, but my modest place will be a chandelier-free zone.*

Two people. That's how I often feel. One believes God for everything and trusts that no matter what, God is good, He is for us, and He is in control. The other panics and wants to protect herself. She is still the little girl who believes she's on her own.

Are you ever like that? Part of you is full of faith, confident in the goodness of God, but there's still a part that panics when things fall apart.

It might be a child who has wandered away from faith. You pray and give that child over to God, but part of you still feels compelled to try to fix her yourself, even though in the past that has made things worse.

It could be the loss of a job. You know the scripture that says God will supply all your need according to His great riches (Phil. 4:19), but has He seen the checking account balance recently?

Perhaps your husband won't come to church with you. You pray for him, believing that God is the only One who can change a heart, but then you fall back into attempting to nag him into the kingdom.

This kind of faith wavering is a dilemma that the great apostle Paul dealt with too. "I have discovered this principle of life," he wrote, "that when I want to do what is right, I inevitably do what is wrong. I love God's law with all my heart. But there is another power within me that is at war with my mind. This power makes me a slave to the sin that is still within me. Oh, what a miserable person I am! Who will free me from this life that is dominated by sin and death?" (Rom. 7:21–24).

It was raining by the time I pulled into the counselor's parking lot. Barry's car was already there, and he'd already gone in. I prayed a prayer I'd never prayed before.

God, please overrule me. Let Your love and grace speak louder than my history.

I opened the office door and went into the counselor's waiting room. (By now you know that I frequent them.) Barry sat on the couch. I joined him on the other end, but I didn't say anything to him. I thought to myself, *I wonder if the counselor would like another sofa, or a nice chandelier?* Magazines were strewn across the table, old copies of *National Geographic* and *Better Homes and Gardens*. I grabbed that one before Barry got any more ideas.

Finally our counselor, a tall man in his sixties, opened his office door and invited us in. He has a kind face, and he always thinks before he speaks. This was our third visit. He asked us both how things had been since our last appointment.

"Fine," I said, "but I've been out of the country, so that probably doesn't count."

He asked Barry how he was doing.

"Terrible," he said. "Every day I wake up knowing the damage I've caused our family. It's like a lead weight in the pit of my stomach."

"That's a lot to bear," the counselor agreed.

"What makes it worse is that I can't fix it," Barry said. "I can change from this point out, but I can't undo the past."

Our counselor was quiet for a moment. Then he spoke. "A man was asked, 'Who is your favorite person on this earth?' The man replied, 'My tailor, because every time he sees me, he takes fresh measurements.'"

No one said anything for a few moments as his words hung in the air between us. Such a simple analogy. The tailor never judged the man by what he was a week ago or a year ago, just how he measured on that day.

That grace-filled image hit us both like a wave of mercy. Barry looked at me with tears in his eyes.

The counselor asked, "Could you be like that tailor, Sheila?"

I knew the answer. "Yes," I said. "I could do that!"

It's hard on paper to convey the impact of that simple picture. There was nothing specifically "Christian" about the analogy, yet for me it embodied the gospel. The apostle Paul would seem to agree: "Anyone who belongs to Christ has become a new person. The old life is gone; a new life has begun!" (2 Cor. 5:17).

If Christ has removed our sin beyond reach, how could I do any less? If Barry's life had been renewed before my eyes, how could I keep reminding him of his shame? God doesn't.

> *For his unfailing love toward those who fear him*
>   *is as great as the height of the heavens above the earth.*
> *He has removed our sins as far from us*
>   *as the east is from the west.*

The Lord is like a father to his children,

tender and compassionate to those who fear him."

(Ps. 103:11–13)

David wrote this psalm from a deep place, from a place of understanding grace. Often we think that grace is a New Testament concept, but from Genesis to Revelation grace abounds.

Grasping hold of the truth that one psalm alone contains could alter the trajectory of your life. Fresh measurements . . . the image stayed with me. There are times in life when I'm deeply impacted by a moment, but it doesn't last. This was not one of those. For me the tailor is a picture of grace. Every time grace opens the door to us, it's as if we are meeting for the very first time. God doesn't hold on to how we failed a year ago or even last night. When we've confessed our sin, it's gone, and we get to begin again.

I don't know what weighs you down. I don't know what regrets you have, but I know this: until you're able to allow grace to wash over you in wave after wave, you won't be able to share that kind of grace with anyone else. Grace is particular to Christianity. There's no other system of religious belief in the past or present that contains such a weighty emphasis on divine grace. Some of the more radical religions even require their followers to die for their faith to prove their obedience. *Only in Christianity did our God die for us to prove His grace.*

Although we say we believe in the amazing grace of God and have sung the hymn for years, our behavior doesn't always back up our beliefs. I think we find grace in its purest form a little off-putting. Grace is offensive to us because it's not fair.

God is not fair. God is grace. He graces us with what we don't deserve: His forgiveness and love.

Do you remember the story Jesus told about the injustice of grace? It's an extensive passage but worth looking at here because it perfectly illustrates how we struggle with grace.

For the Kingdom of Heaven is like the landowner who went out early one morning to hire workers for his vineyard. He agreed to pay the normal daily wage and sent them out to work.

At nine o'clock in the morning he was passing through the market-place and saw some people standing around doing nothing. So he hired them, telling them he would pay them whatever was right at the end of the day. So they went to work in the vineyard. At noon and again at three o'clock he did the same thing.

At five o'clock that afternoon he was in town again and saw some more people standing around. He asked them, "Why haven't you been working today?"

They replied, "Because no one hired us."

The landowner told them, "Then go out and join the others in my vineyard."

That evening he told the foreman to call the workers in and pay them, beginning with the last workers first. When those hired at five o'clock were paid, each received a full day's wage. When those hired first came to get their pay, they assumed they would receive more. But they, too, were paid a day's wage. When they received their pay, they protested to the owner, "Those people worked only one hour, and yet you've paid them just as much as you paid us who worked all day in the scorch-ing heat."

He answered one of them, "Friend, I haven't been unfair! Didn't you agree to work all day for the usual wage? Take your money and go. I wanted to pay this last worker the same as you. Is it against the law for me to do what I want with my money? Should you be jealous because I am kind to others?"

So those who are last now will be first then, and those who are first will be last. (Matt. 20:1–16)

We don't like that, do we? It just seems wrong.

How can someone show up at the last minute and receive exactly as much as the one who's been out in the field, sweating, since sunrise?

How can "that woman" who broke up your marriage and then supposedly repented and asked for forgiveness be as welcomed at communion as you are?

How can a murderer find salvation in Christ moments before his execution and be as welcomed into heaven as those who have served Him faithfully all their lives?

How can one of two thieves being executed on either side of the sinless Lamb of God hear this radical news with moments left to live: "I assure you, today you will be with me in paradise?" (Luke 23:43).

God's love has never been based on our behavior, good or bad. It's always been based on His nature. So how do we begin to really grasp that? Understanding grace is the work of God in our lives, and we each walk our own journey to understanding it. Mine came in a small Episcopal church in Washington, DC, at the lowest point in my life.

I had given my life to Christ as an eleven-year-old and was very involved in church through my teen years. I never rebelled, more out of fear than faith. I didn't want God to stop loving me the way it seemed my dad had. I went to seminary, joined Youth for Christ, and then moved to America. I worked with Dr. Billy Graham in his crusades and then spent five years as cohost of *The 700 Club*.

My point in reiterating all that is I never really saw my need for grace. It made sense to me that if you engaged in sexual sin or drank like a fish or stuffed things up your nose other than a Kleenex, then, of course, you needed grace. I was just a scared little good girl. Why did I need grace?

It was only when I sat in the back row of that Washington, DC, church one September morning in 1992 that I began to finally understand. As I sat there, out on a day pass from the psych hospital, with everything that I'd worked so hard to maintain in ruins at my feet, the words of a hymn my nana used to sing to me as a child rang out inside my broken heart.

> *Nothing in my hands I bring*
> *Simply to thy cross I cling*
> *Naked, come to Thee for dress*
> *Helpless, look to Thee for grace*
> *Foul, I to the fountain fly*
> *Wash me, Savior, or I die[2]*

I finally got it. Nothing in my hands I bring—nothing! I'd been coming to God with hands full of the things I'd done for Him for years. It's an exhausting, punishing way to live, but to simply cling to the cross . . . that is grace.

I'm not the good news. Jesus is.

I never had been and never would be. Grace has always been about Jesus. Amazing how sometimes God will take you to a prison (or a psychiatric ward) to set you free.

As I sat in our counselor's office that day in the winter of 2015, when the counselor asked, "Could you do that, Sheila?" the reason I said yes with everything in me was I finally remembered what I had forgotten. I recalled the grace that had loved me back to life in 1992. So how could I say no to Barry?

I love when the Holy Spirit prompts our hearts and minds and, in a moment, the path ahead is clear. I wonder if that's what happened to King David? Of all the stories of grace found in God's Word, the one, apart from the cross of Christ, that moves me most is found tucked deep into the heart of David's story. It's an obscure passage about a man whose name I still can't pronounce, Mephibosheth. His story is found in 2 Samuel 9 during the highest point in David's reign, right before his sin with Bathsheba.

The Israelite army had destroyed thousands of its enemies. "In fact," we read, "the LORD made David victorious wherever he went" (2 Sam. 8:14). Israel had never been stronger. As David took time to reflect on the past, he remembered the promise he had made to his best friend, Jonathan.

Do you remember the incident in the field, when Jonathan told David he would send a sign by arrows to let him know whether it was safe to come back to the palace or not? "If [my father] speaks favorably about you," he said, "I will let you know. But if he is angry and wants you killed, may the LORD strike me and even kill me if I don't warn you so you can escape and live. May the LORD be with you as he used to be with my father. And may you treat me with the faithful love of the LORD as long as I live. But if I die, treat my family with this faithful love, even when the LORD destroys all your enemies from the face of the earth" (1 Sam. 20:12–15).

It was the custom in those days that when a new king ascended the throne, all the descendants of the previous king were slaughtered to remove even the possibility of a revolt. Jonathan asked David to show grace to his family where none was legislated. David said he would.

Not only had David made a promise to his beloved friend; he also made a promise to Saul, Jonathan's father. "And now I realize that you are surely going to be king," Saul had told him, "and that the kingdom of Israel will flourish under your rule. Now swear to me by the LORD that when that happens you will not kill my family and destroy my line of descendants!" The Bible tells us that "David promised this to Saul with an oath" (1 Sam. 24:20–22).

Keeping a promise like that would have meant little to Saul, but David was a man of his word. What could he do now to honor his promise? Saul and Jonathan were dead. As far as David knew, there were no survivors in their line. Still, David determined to find out. "Is anyone in Saul's family still alive—anyone to whom I can show kindness for Jonathan's sake?" (2 Sam. 9:1). Do you see the grace tucked in there? He didn't ask if there was anyone noble left; he asked if there was *anyone*. Grace says, "Come as you are."

David called for Ziba, one of Saul's former servants, and asked him if he knew of anyone from Saul's line who was still alive. "Yes," Ziba told him, "one of Jonathan's sons is still alive. He is crippled in both feet" (9:3). I wonder why he told him that detail. Was he trying to let David know that this crippled man wouldn't fit in his lovely palace? This man Mephibosheth was the only survivor of King Saul's line. He had suffered a lot over his lifetime.

In 2 Samuel 4:4 we find out what happened to him: "[Mephibosheth] was five years old when the report came from Jezreel that Saul and Jonathan had been killed in battle. When the child's nurse heard the news, she picked him up and fled. But as she hurried away, she dropped him, and he became crippled." Can you imagine the scene? The nurse knew nothing of the promise made to Saul or to Jonathan. When she heard that they were both dead, she just knew she had to spirit the boy out of the palace before David's men would kill the one who would now be heir to the throne. We don't know if she tripped or he struggled, but he fell so hard that he broke his legs and had been crippled ever since.

Mephibosheth lived in a place called Lo-Debar, which translates as "no pastureland." For years he had been hidden away in a grassless place until grace would come looking for him. I can't imagine what he must have thought when David's men knocked at the door. Perhaps, like me, he had spent years waiting for the other shoe to drop, waiting to be discovered, and now what he dreaded had come to pass. The men took him to Jerusalem, right into the king's palace. Mephibosheth bowed low to the ground, expecting the worst. We know that because of David's response, "Don't be afraid!" He went on to say, "I intend to show kindness to you because of my promise to your father, Jonathan. I will give you all the property that once belonged to your grandfather Saul, and you will eat here with me at the king's table!" (2 Sam. 9:7).

He could see the fear etched on this broken man's face, but grace soaked the crippled man to the skin. Not only would his life be spared, everything that used to belong to his grandfather would now be his. But grace was even greater than this. He was offered a seat at King David's table. He was welcomed home, as family.

Isn't that what we all want? We want to be wanted, to belong, and to be given what we know we don't deserve but long for. Can you imagine the scene at dinnertime? David is seated at the head; Amnon sits there with Absalom, Tamar, and Solomon, and then, as Chuck Swindoll wrote, "They hear this clump, clump, clump, clump, and here comes Mephibosheth hobbling along. He smiles and humbly joins the others as he takes his place at the table as one of the king's sons. And the tablecloth of grace covers his feet."[3]

What a beautiful picture! Just as David, out of love for Jonathan, lavished grace on his child, so God, out of His great love for Christ, gives us a place at His table as sons and daughters. It's hard to grasp the depth of this kind of welcoming love. We are invited to come just as we are, with our limps and crutches and zero qualifications. David could have restored Saul's wealth to Mephibosheth and sent him off, but he did so much more than that. He made Mephibosheth a son.

When you've been shown that kind of grace, you long to share it with others. As I shared earlier, a couple of weeks after I'd been released from the psychiatric hospital in the early 1990s, Ruth Bell Graham invited me to spend a few days at their North Carolina home. I flew into the Asheville airport. One of their staff picked me up and drove me the thirty minutes to their house set high in the mountains. Ruth met me at the gate and introduced me to their two German shepherds. Apparently it was important that they knew I was a friend. Amen to that!

It was a lovely afternoon, so we sat outside in rocking chairs, drinking iced tea and enjoying the quiet. Ruth could see that I was tired, so after dinner she showed me to my bedroom and asked if I'd like a cup of tea. It's a memory that I treasure. There was a high bed with little wooden steps beside it and crisp white linens that Ruth told me she'd bought in Switzerland.

I was tucked up in bed when she came back with my tea and asked if she could read to me. She sat at the bottom of the bed with an old Scottish book, *Beside the Bonnie Brier Bush* by Ian Maclaren. She thumbed through the well-worn pages until she found what she was looking for, "The Transformation of Lachlan Campbell." Ruth asked me if I knew the story, but I didn't. So she said, "It's about a young girl, Flora Campbell, whose mother had died. Her strict, judgmental father, Lachlan, now raised her. Their home was a truly graceless place, so one day Flora ran away to London. Her father was so furious that he removed her name from the family Bible. She was wretched and alone in London."

"One night she made her way into a church," Ruth continued, and she began to read:

> You maybe know that a wounded deer will try to hide herself, and I crept into the shadow of a church, and wept. Then the people and the noise and the houses passed away like the mist on the hill, and I was walking to the kirk with my father, oh yes, and I saw you all in your places, and I heard the Psalms, and I could see through the window the green fields and the trees on the edge of the moor. And I saw my home, with the dogs before the door, and the flowers that I planted, and the lamb coming for her milk, and I heard myself singing, and I awoke. But there was singing, oh yes, and beautiful too, for the dark church was open, and the light was falling over my head . . . and this was the hymn—"There is a fountain filled with blood."

Ruth paused for a moment. "Life is unbearable without grace," she said. "They both needed it, the daughter and the father. This is my favorite part, when Flora makes her way home." She continued to read:

> When she reached the door, her strength had departed, and she was not able to knock. But there was no need, for the dogs, who never forget nor cast off, were bidding her welcome with short joyous yelps of delight, and she could hear her father feeling for the latch, which for once could not be found, and saying nothing but "Flora, Flora."
>
> She had made up some kind of speech, but the only word she ever said was "Father," for Lachlan, who had never even kissed her all the days of her youth, clasped her in his arms and sobbed out blessings over her head, while the dogs licked her hands with their soft, kindly tongues.[4]

I'll never forget that night or the grace that was lavished all over me by Ruth. As I left, she gave me her copy of the book.

When I got home from our time with the counselor that day in 2015, I picked up Ruth's book and turned once more through the well-worn pages until I found Lachlan and Flora's story. It ends like this:

> *Flora Campbell.*
> Missed April 1873.
> Found September 1873.
> "Her father fell on her neck and kissed her."[5]

Flora's is the story of the prodigal son. It's the story of the lost daughter. It's the story of anyone who longs for grace, and when grace finds you, you can't keep it to yourself. It has to ring out like church bells: *I was lost but now I'm found.* I knew I had been forgiven so much, and like a girl soaking up her father's praise, I longed to stay in that place so I could then lavish that same grace and kindness on Barry, to let him start fresh and clean. I'd been given that exact gift right before I met him. That kind of grace changed the trajectory of my life, made me who I would become.

The truth is, because I've been so radically graced, I don't want to live graceless. Is it hard to see Barry as the tailor sees him, to measure him today instead of bringing up the baggage of the past? Yes, it is hard. But in that counseling office, I grabbed my husband's hand and made a promise. And by God's grace, I intend to keep it.

The Longing for God Alone

O God, you are my God;
    I earnestly search for you.
My soul thirsts for you;
    my whole body longs for you
in this parched and weary land
    where there is no water.
I have seen you in your sanctuary
    and gazed upon your power and glory.
Your unfailing love is better than life itself;
    how I praise you!
    —*Psalm 63:1–3*

And this God, the living God, your God, our God,
    is in me, is in you, lives in us, and we live and move
and have our being in Him. And He is in us by virtue
    of the hunger, the longing, which we have for Him.
He is Himself creating the longing for Himself.[1]
    —*Miguel de Unamuno*

HIS NAME IS BIG BILLY. HE'S THE TEDDY BEAR
I've had since I was two, and he smiles down at me from the second shelf
of the bookcase in my study as I write. I believe he used to have fur, but

now, as with the Skin Horse in *The Velveteen Rabbit*, it's all been "loved off." He used to speak when you squeezed his tummy, but he hasn't said a word in years.

I've lived in five countries and many more homes, and along the way, furniture styles have changed, lifestyle has been minimized or enlarged, bags of stuff have been donated to the Salvation Army, but Big Billy remains. He is one of the few things, after my family and dogs, I would grab if we were ever threatened by fire. Sometimes I wish he could speak. I know I whispered things to him as a child that I'd love to remember now. Do you have a Big Billy? Perhaps for you it was a blanket or some other toy?

My very first tour of America in the late eighties was with legendary guitarist Phil Keaggy. His wife, Bernadette, and first daughter, Alicia, traveled with us. She was two. Everywhere Alicia went, Miss Mousey accompanied her. She dragged this beloved mouse in a dress through puddles, spilled juice on her, and had subjected the poor stuffed mouse to the many rigors of life on the road. Concerned that Miss Mousey might get lost along the way, Bernadette bought a backup Miss Mousey.

One day she removed the real M. M. and put the imposter in Alicia's bed on the bus to see if she'd be accepted. I'm sure Alicia's grandmother heard her screams in Youngstown, Ohio. "This is not my Miss Mousey!" The mouse looked so much better than the original, but it wasn't hers.

Why do you think we do that as children? Why do we cling to one thing that brings us such comfort? I believe that it is the earliest sign that we long for God. We are born with an innate longing deep inside to connect to something or someone who understands us completely. It's a longing that began in the garden of Eden. When the perfect, intimate relationship that Adam and Eve shared with God broke, the longing began. Before that devastating moment, there was no longing because God walked with us in the cool of the evening. Life in fellowship with our Creator was as it was supposed to be. Our hearts had no gaping hole because God was everything to us. He walked with us. That distant memory still courses through our DNA.

There is a quotation that's been ascribed to G. K. Chesterton, St. Francis, and St. Augustine, but the only documented source of this quotation I can find is in the book *The World, The Flesh, and Father Smith* by Bruce Marshall (1945). It reads, "The young man who rings the bell at the brothel is unconsciously looking for God."[2] The first time I heard a speaker share that quote, I thought, *What a bunch of baloney! That's just a nice way for a man to justify his lust by saying, "Yep, I saw the red light, but really, I was just looking for Jesus!"* But the more I've sat with it, the more I believe it's true. I believe we search for God with all our longings and all our lusts.

The woman who has a hundred pairs of shoes in her closet is longing for more than foot fashion.

The one who reaches for another drink until the day is obliterated is longing for more than just an alcohol-induced coma.

When you shove one more cookie into your mouth that no longer even tastes good, it's not because you are hungry for cookies; you are hungering for more.

The one who takes another pain pill after the original pain is gone is trying to quiet a pain that will never permanently respond to medication.

When one disappointing relationship leads to another and another, yet you keep moving on, perhaps it's not that you haven't met Mr. Right yet, but the One you long for is above them all.

Every longing that we try to satisfy apart from God will always fall short because, as Augustine of Hippo wrote, "You have made us for Yourself, O Lord, and our heart is restless until it rests in You."[3]

That almost seems a little sneaky of God. He placed us in a world surrounded by a million and one temptations, knowing that not one of them will ever fully satisfy us apart from Him. It's either sneaky or the most radically beautiful love story ever told. Just as God in Christ pursued us through the mud and mire, the beatings and the bloody path up to a cross, He calls us now to pursue Him. Not only that: He promises that if we seek Him, we will find Him. So this is not a cruel joke. This is not a lab technician crossing a dance floor on a dare and leaving the seventeen-year-old misfit that I was with one more reason not to trust. No, this is a promise written in the Lamb's blood.

"'For I know the plans I have for you,' declares the LORD, 'plans to prosper you and not to harm you, plans to give you hope and a future. Then you will call on me and come and pray to me, and I will listen to you. You will seek me and find me when you seek me with all your heart. I will be found by you,' declares the LORD" (Jer. 29:11–14 NIV).

That's a beautiful promise, and I believe it. It's one thing to believe that something is true; it's quite another to live, to stay, to remain in its truth. I have believed that what Augustine wrote is true for most of my adult life. I just haven't known what to do with it. How do you rest in God? What does that even mean? Honestly, that's what led to writing this book. I know that underneath the rubble of the chapters of my story, the true longing of my heart is for God and Him alone.

I've traveled around the world during the last thirty years and spoken to more than five million women. I know I'm not alone in this quest to understand how to rest in God. I've listened as you've graciously shared parts of your stories with me. I see the common thread running through our lives, the longing and the ache for more of Him. Like me, we're just not quite sure how to get there. I've seen devastating paths that some have walked. The consequences are greater for some than for others.

If you believed that love and desire were what you needed to feel whole, that longing may have cost you your marriage or your self-respect.

If you believed that more stuff would make you feel better, then credit card debt might hang around your neck like a millstone.

If food seemed to offer the comfort, friendship, and intimacy you lack, then your own body may have become the prison, the wall around your life.

If you thought having children would fill the emptiness inside, you may be deeply disappointed because you expected them to be what only God can be to you.

There are so many more scenarios I could write, but you know your story, your hopes, your longings, and the path you've taken until this moment in life. The reason I listed some here is I want to acknowledge that we all have longings, and though some lead to greater heartache than others, we're all the same. None of us are alone in this universal need. *Jesus came because we are all messed up—not because some of us are more messed up than others.*

Would you sit with that for just a moment? It's easy to say that we agree we're all messed up and give that truth a "Like" on Instagram or Facebook, but do we live as if we believe that's true? We all seem to possess an internal set of the scales of justice. If you were well-loved as a child, you may extend more mercy to yourself and to others. But if those early years were either bereft of love or scarred by the wrong kind of love, I'm pretty sure you've spent quite a few of your adult years beating yourself up. The trouble with trying to make yourself pay for something that wasn't your fault is you don't know when you're done.

Men seem to wear their insecurities through sports or cars or the blond on their arm. But women display insecurity by deciding who is "in" and who is "out." As you know, women can be very cruel to each other. We love to point fingers and judge the thing that we're not tempted by as if it's a greater sin than the one we hide. In other words, we judge relentlessly those who sin differently than we do. Do we hope that it will make us feel better about ourselves? Judging others won't make us feel better. Not only that, but someday we may need the very mercy we now withhold.

As an itinerant singer and speaker, I was somewhat protected from the world of women and the ways we deal with each other—until Christian went to school. Then I grew acutely aware of the little groups women like to form and the way we talk about each other. I'd love to say that this situation is different among Christian women, but in most places, it's not. As God's loved daughters, we need to be shaken to our core, to our knees, until we begin to grasp the price that's been paid for our redemption. Perhaps then this world will see what God's love looks like by the way we treat each other. We live in a day when young people are leaving the church in droves. In 2012, the Pew Research Center published "Nones, on the Rise," where they reported that a third of all Americans under thirty said their religious affiliation was "None."[4]

Perhaps our hypocrisy in chasing things other than Jesus has sent them running? Unless we have been radicalized by the cross, we will inevitably be radicalized by something else, whether money or relationships or status or our own brand of holiness. Only the cross calls us higher, yet takes us to our knees, to live lives of self-denial, elevating the needs of others. Only a vision of the greatness of God causes us to relinquish our pursuit of things and, instead, kneel at His feet.

During his lifetime King David watched his kingdom rise to the heights promised to Abraham. Heady days, those. He defeated vast armies and watched as God interfered with the plans of those who attempted to take him out, restoring him once more to the throne of Israel. David allowed his longings to lead him into the kind of sin that caused death and devastation to others. Humbling days. Yet Paul, the great apostle, said, "God testified concerning him: 'I have found David son of Jesse, a man after my own heart; he will do everything I want him to do'" (Acts 13:22 NIV).

As we've turned through the pages of David's life, we've seen sin, but we've also seen humility, worship, trust, hope, repentance, strength, and love. The greatest gift of King David's life to me is this: his absolute trust in the goodness and mercy of God no matter what raged around him. David's story reminds me that it's not how you start life that matters; it's how you finish. When Samuel the prophet came to anoint the next king, you'll remember that David's father didn't even think to include him. He was just the boy in the field with the sheep. I was just the girl who walked in her sleep and had nightmares that her dad wasn't really dead and would come back and finish her off.

What about you? What occurred in the first couple of chapters of your life that has caused you to count yourself out? I believe that's going to change. As I travel around the world, I see that God is raising up a ragtag army of women. We don't look like much to be concerned with, but we are mighty. We are the ones who are tired of listening to the enemy's no about our lives and are ready to believe God's yes!

Saying yes is the passionate pursuit for the rest of my life, this calling of God's daughters to live a better story, a bigger life. Whatever your path has looked like up until this point (unless there is a white chalk mark around your body), it's not too late to change, to rise up and be the woman God has called and created you to be. You are not defined by the past. You are qualified by the great I Am.

As I charted the course of this manuscript, I did so with an awareness of several things in my life. I knew that the longings I've had in the past for protection or closure have led to dark, difficult, and dead-end places. Anytime I've expected to find complete fulfillment in another person or situation, I have always experienced disappointment. I know, too, that the desperate desire of my heart is to navigate through the maze of this messy world to find the One who loves me as I long to be loved. Those two realities have driven me. I'm not one who writes as an expert on a subject. I'm one who writes out of a hunger to understand.

I love my husband, Barry. We've been through a lot of tough stuff, but I love him. I love him now for different reasons than I did twenty years ago.

Recently my friend Lisa Whelchel and I were speaking at an event at Tim Keller's Redeemer Church in downtown New York. We grabbed a little alone time in the dressing room to catch up with each other. She is not a fan of small talk and loves to ask direct questions. So she asked this, "What do you love most about Barry?"

I thought for a moment. Twenty years ago I would have said that I loved his looks, his sense of humor, and his creativity. That night my answer was none of those things. I told Lisa, "I love that he tells the truth and owns it when he has messed up."

That's a huge gift. I don't think we can ask much more from each other than that. Sure, it would be nice if we never messed up, but check your address. Unless "Streets of Gold, Fourth Mansion to the Left" is there, we're not home yet. Barry will accept nothing less from me. When something is clearly my issue, I own it and ask God to help me live differently.

As I sit at my desk today and look back on my life, I see two inescapable things: the brokenness of my choices and the faithfulness of God. I so want you to see this, girls! In the worst days of my life, living with the poorest choices I could have ever made, God was there. He never left me. He never sat back and said, "Well, you did it again. That was your last chance!" He's never left you either—never did and never will. His love for us isn't based on our perfect performance, but on the perfect love He has for us.

If I could summarize my heart in this book about longing, it would be with this: God is for you 100 percent. He loves you and welcomes you just as you are. He will never turn away from you, never be too busy, never stop listening, and never choose to be with someone else rather than you. One of the attributes of our great Father is that He is omnipresent. He is with you right now just as He is with me. But unless you believe that, you'll never trust Him with your deepest longings. Instead you will try to satisfy your longing outside of who He is and what He provides.

So that's the choice. Will you believe?

But don't take my word for it on how crazy God is about you; let's see what Jesus had to say.

Do you remember the story Jesus told about three lost things? The lost sheep, the lost coin, and the lost boy? (Two lost boys, really, but we'll look at that in a moment.) Those stories are found in Luke 15, a chapter often referred to as "the gospel in the gospel."[5] The sheep wandered off, the coin disappeared, and one of the boys deliberately walked off while the other stayed right where he was. Christ's message to everyone listening that day was radical and unambiguous: whether you wandered away from God, fell away, or decided you'd had enough and turned and walked away, God would never stop pursuing you.

Let's place the story in context. The religious leaders and teachers of the day found Christ's behavior deeply troubling. It's one thing to toss a coin at a beggar, quite another to look him in the eyes and talk to him, ridiculously unacceptable to sit and eat with them. Sharing a meal together is personal and intimate because it puts you on the same level as the one with whom you break bread. Pharisees had a categorization for sinners who didn't keep the Law (some things never change). They called them "the People of the Land."

In his commentary *The Gospel of Luke*, William Barclay wrote on the strict code to which the Pharisees adhered. "When a man is one of the People of the Land, entrust no money to him, take no testimony from him, trust him with no secret, do not appoint him guardian of an orphan, do not make him custodian of charitable funds, do not accompany him on a journey."[6]

The more we learn about the customs and ways of Christ's daily life, the more we understand how radical the story was. Luke, the doctor, one of Christ's followers who would have had some social standing in the pompous crowd, saw the hypocrisy in bearing the name of religion, but not the heart. "Tax collectors and other notorious sinners often came to listen to Jesus teach. This made the Pharisees and teachers of religious law complain that he was associating with such sinful people—even eating with them!" (Luke 15:1–2).

Christ, the consummate storyteller, began the story of three lost things with the story of a lost sheep:

> "If a man has a hundred sheep and one of them gets lost, what will he do? Won't he leave the ninety-nine others in the wilderness and go to search for the one that is lost until he finds it? And when he has found it, he will joyfully carry it home on his shoulders. When he arrives, he will call together his friends and neighbors, saying, 'Rejoice with me because I have found my lost sheep.' In the same way, there is more joy in heaven over one lost sinner who repents and returns to God than over ninety-nine others who are righteous and haven't strayed away!" (Luke 15:4–7)

This was a shocking and offensive story to the strictest-of-the-strict Jews. According to Barclay's commentary, they lived by the code "There is joy in heaven over one sinner who is obliterated before God."[7] Even to those who believed that God would receive a sinner who came to Him in the right way, this was a radical, brand-new teaching. The idea that God would actually be the one to initiate the search was unheard-of. Not only that, the story was about joy!

Shepherds knew their sheep well. It wasn't unusual for one to wander off, but rarely did they find their way back. In this story Christ introduced His listeners to His Father in a way they had never dared to imagine. It seemed too good to be true. He told the scribes and Pharisees, knowing the bruised and broken were listening, that if one of His sheep wandered off, God would not only go looking for that one, but He'd also carry it home and invite others to join the celebration when He found it. Unheard-of! Our God likes to party! Over us!

This story is deeply personal to me. My father had a beautiful voice. One of his friends once told me, "It was the kind of voice that made you want to love God more." His favorite hymn to perform was "The Ninety and Nine." After my dad's death it was very hard for my mum to listen to that hymn. I dreaded seeing that number appear on the hymn board in our church when I was growing up, knowing that Mum would cry her way through it. It wasn't the crying that was the hardest part; it was that we never really talked about what happened with my father. It was just something terrible that had happened in the past, and we had moved on.

I didn't even know where my dad was buried.

Years later, after I was released from the psychiatric hospital, I flew home to Scotland. There were so many missing pieces from the puzzle of my early life that I wanted to place back together. Though I wanted to honor my mum and not stir things up, I desperately needed some closure for myself. So I visited the place where my dad's life ended. I didn't know the exact spot, just that he had escaped from the hospital one night and drowned himself in the river.

It was a cold, damp day as I drove the rental car through the gates of the hospital to the parking area at the side. I got out of the car and pulled the collar of my coat up around my neck to keep some of the wind away. I made my way through the grass down to the edge of the river. I don't know what I was looking for. Understanding? Regret? Sadness? I've no idea. What I didn't expect to find? Hope. As I stood at the edge and looked into the clear, moving water, I felt the presence of Christ with me. The words of the hymn that had haunted my teenage years now brought comfort, particularly these two verses written by Elizabeth C. Clephane in 1868:

> But none of the ransomed ever knew
> How deep were the waters crossed;
> Nor how dark was the night the Lord passed through
> Ere He found His sheep that was lost.
> Out in the desert He heard its cry,

Sick and helpless and ready to die;
Sick and helpless and ready to die.

And all through the mountains, thunder riven
And up from the rocky steep,
There arose a glad cry to the gate of Heaven,
"Rejoice! I have found My sheep!"
And the angels echoed around the throne,
"Rejoice, for the Lord brings back His own!
Rejoice, for the Lord brings back His own!"[8]

I believe that in His great mercy Christ met my father that dark night, wounded in mind and spirit, lost and sick and helpless, and carried him home. What did my dad long for that night? I'm sure just one thing: home. In that homecoming, he finally learned that the love of God is far greater than his wounds, far wider than his desperate wandering.

Outrageous, you think? That's certainly what the religious leaders would have believed. How are you supposed to get people to toe the line with that kind of grace-laced message? But Jesus wasn't done. More love would come, because next he told a story about a lost coin: "Or suppose a woman has ten silver coins and loses one. Won't she light a lamp and sweep the entire house and search carefully until she finds it? And when she finds it, she will call in her friends and neighbors and say, 'Rejoice with me because I have found my lost coin.' In the same way, there is joy in the presence of God's angels when even one sinner repents" (Luke 15:8–10).

The lost coin might feel like a smaller stake here, but it was worth about one day's working wage to a man. To the woman who lost it, however, it represented far more. The mark of a married woman in those days was ten silver coins on a silver chain that she wore around her head. To lose one of those would be like losing a wedding ring.

I lost my wedding ring six years ago. I still haven't found it, and I still haven't given up. I think it probably went out with the trash. Although we're only a family of three plus three dogs, we produce enough trash for a small country. On the day that I noticed it missing, I dragged our three trash cans onto the grass in our back garden and emptied them out. It was a horrible job sorting through spent tea bags, eggshells, and soggy bread crusts, all to no avail. Even now, if I put on something I haven't worn for a while, I check the pockets and the lining, hoping against hope to find it.

In Christ's story the woman with the lost coin won't rest until she's found it. Christ tucks another spiritual nugget into this shorter story about salvation. "Rejoice with me because I have found my lost coin" (Luke 15:9). Do you see the beauty of ownership here? *My* lost coin! To those who had been made to feel like outsiders for so long, God in Christ now owns them, not in a property way, but as a loving father takes care of his children.

Yet again Jesus took this truth to an even deeper level with the story of the prodigal son. I used to think this was a story about an ungrateful son who ran away, but now I understand it's the story of a party, a great big glorious party that God has thrown for all who will dare to come and partake!

Perhaps it seems strange that we're ending this book on longing unpacking three stories found in Luke's gospel. After all, King David is not in Luke's gospel. I beg to differ. I'll show you why, because I don't have a single doubt that King David is at this very party.

In his lovely book *Come to the Party*, Karl Olsson says that if you attempt to spread the message that the gospel is a great big God-ordained party, you'll discover people will fall into one of four groups:

1. Those who doubt that there is a party.
2. Those who believe that there is a party somewhere, but they're not invited.

3. Those who believe there is a party and they're invited but they
   don't deserve to stay.
4. Those who are invited and go and stay.⁹

If the first two stories raised the Pharisees' blood pressure, this final one must have caused a stroke. The story went against everything that made sense to good, religious, righteous people. Then again, Jesus didn't hang out with those kinds of people. As Holden Caulfield said in *The Catcher in the Rye* (referring to Christ's disciples), "They were alright after Jesus was dead and all, but while he was alive, they were about as much use to him as a hole in the head."¹⁰

"To illustrate the point further, Jesus told them this story: 'A man had two sons. The younger son told his father, "I want my share of your estate now before you die." So his father agreed to divide his wealth between his sons'" (Luke 15:11–12).

This story is the most offensive of all. You can understand a sheep wandering off or a coin falling off with the rapid turn of a head, but this boy, this one is selfish, arrogant, with no regard for his father's feelings. He's basically saying, "I'd love to stay around until you die, but goodness knows how long that will take, so I'm out of here!" If I'd been that boy's mother, I would have smacked him so hard he would have been hearing "Jingle Bells" for several Christmases to come!

So right from the start the hearers don't like this story. The Pharisees are already thinking that this father deserves no sympathy. By law he should have simply disowned the son and been done with him. But Jesus went on:

"A few days later this younger son packed all his belongings and moved to a distant land, and there he wasted all his money in wild living. About the time his money ran out, a great famine swept over the land, and he began to starve. He persuaded a local farmer to hire him, and the man sent him into his fields to feed the pigs. The young man became so hungry that even the pods he was feeding the pigs looked good to him" (Luke 15:13–16).

Finally the story had some redemptive purpose as far as the Pharisees could tell. Perfect end to a dreadful story . . . a Jewish boy insults his father and ends up in a Jewish nightmare, feeding pigs! But Jesus didn't stop there.

"When he finally came to his senses, he said to himself, 'At home even the hired servants have food enough to spare, and here I am dying of hunger! I will go home to my father and say, "Father, I have sinned against both heaven and you, and I am no longer worthy of being called your son. Please take me on as a hired servant" ' " (vv. 17–19).

Ridiculous!

Can't you hear the crowd muttering?

Didn't come home because he was sorry but because he was hungry!

Send him packing!

Ungrateful wretch!

But wait! The story is far from over.

"And while he was still a long way off, his father saw him coming. Filled with love and compassion, he ran to his son, embraced him, and kissed him" (v. 20).

I'm pretty sure the crowd grew angry now. Luke didn't tell us. He was such a doctor, just the minimum amount of information and no more! For a respected father to pick up his robes and run would be unheard-of. For such a father to run to the son who had insulted him would be out-rageous and unthinkable. That was the very point.

God's love is outrageous.

God's love is unthinkable.

God's love makes no sense.

God's love is like God's love and no one else's.

Which is why the prodigal's brother didn't like it.

It's also why a large percentage of the church doesn't like it either, because it's not . . . fair. Yes, there we go again. God's love is not fair.

"All these years I've slaved for you and never once refused to do a single thing you told me to," the older son complained. "And in all that time you never gave me even one young goat for a feast with my friends. Yet when this son of yours comes back after squandering your money on prostitutes, you celebrate by killing the fattened calf!" (15:29–30).

Underneath all that good behavior, rage lurks. Both sons were pretty messed up. It was just more obvious with one than the other. I was the older brother for years. I was the one who did all the right things for the wrong reasons. The story really isn't about the boys; it's about their father. If we miss that, we've missed the whole point. From Genesis to Revelation, the story's not really been about us; it's been about our Father. Some of us ran off and partied. Some stayed home and were responsible. But we aren't the heroes of the story—the Father is. He waits for all of us.

All the time the "bad" son was away, the "good" son could have simply enjoyed being with his dad, hanging out with him at the gate, watching the road or the sun go down. He could have joined him on the back porch, shared a cup of coffee as the sun began to rise on another day. But he was too busy getting life right. In reality, he wanted what his dad had just as much as the other brother. He also missed that what his dad wanted was for the boys to want to be with him. He wanted relationship.

"All these years I've slaved for you!" (15:29). He missed the point!

What the father was looking for was a man after his own heart.

Perhaps the fields were a better preparation to understand what God is looking for than a palace ever could be. David must have felt so small on clear nights as he looked up at the stars and sang out his songs to the heavens, but the relationship that began there took him through to the very last song he ever sang:

He reached down from heaven and rescued me;
  he drew me out of deep waters.
He rescued me from my powerful enemies,
  from those who hated me and were too strong for me.
They attacked me at a moment when I was in distress,
  but the LORD supported me.
He led me to a place of safety;
  he rescued me because he delights in me."

(2 Sam. 22:17–20)

He rescued me because He delights in me, according to David.

That's the whole gospel in a nutshell.

He rescued us because He delights in us, not because we got it right and not because we got it wrong. Simply because He delights in us and invites us to delight in Him.

Big Billy knew my secrets and seemed to love me anyway. And while I transferred my longing and affection from him to things, people, anything that I thought would satisfy, Jesus was throwing an amazing grace party, and I was on the invitation. He knew me—flaws and all—and still wanted to spend time with me. So much more than a trusted stuffed animal that couldn't speak, Jesus has proven Himself to me countless times. My longing has been redirected to Him, and He has filled me. My hole-pocked heart is overflowing, knowing that this broken girl now has a home and a party to go to.

You might want to dust off your party dress, show up, and stay for the party, too, friend.

ACKNOWLEDGMENTS

I AM DEEPLY INDEBTED TO LYSA TERKEURST and the Compel Team for their creative input at the beginning of this project. You are brilliant and generous in everything you do.

Thank you to Kristen Parrish for your invaluable editorial input and legendary patience.

Thank you to Janene MacIvor for the love and care you give to each project we have worked on together.

Thank you to Mary DeMuth for helping me to say what's on my heart with clarity and passion.

Thank you to Brian Hampton and your editorial team for your support and invaluable input.

Thank you to Jeff James, Stephanie Tresner, and Tiffany Sawyer for lending your marketing expertise to this project.

Thank you to Kristen Ingebretson and Mallory Collins for creating a wonderful cover and interior design.

Thank you to Esther Fedorkevich and the Fedd Agency for your vision, care, and passion.

Thank you to James and Betty Robison for your love and support. I am deeply grateful to be called by God to work side by side with you at *Life Today* and *The Stream*.

Thank you to my husband, Barry, and son, Christian. You bring so much joy and love to my life.

NOTES

Epigraph

1. C. S. Lewis, *The Weight of Glory and Other Addresses*, HarperCollins e-books.

Introduction

1. George Eliot, *Mill on the Floss, Silas Marner, The Lifted Veil, and Brother Jacob* (Chicago, New York, San Francisco: Belford, Clarke & Co., 1889), 288. This quote is from *The Mill on the Floss*.
2. T. S. Eliot, "Little Gidding," sec. 5, in *Four Quartets* (New York: Harcourt, 1971), 59.

Chapter 1: The Longing to Be Chosen

1. Mike Colaw, "Column: The Deepest Longing of the Human Heart," *Current in Fishers*, June 3, 2014, http://currentinfishers.com/column-deepest-longing -human-heart/.
2. Marc Stein, *Twilight Exposed! The Inside Story of a Billion-Dollar Franchise* (Marc Stein, 2011), 271.
3. G. Frederick Owen, *Abraham to the Middle-East Crisis* (Grand Rapids: Eerdmans, 1939, 1957), 45.

Chapter 2: The Longing to Be Protected

1. Sigmund Freud, *Civilization and Its Discontents* (New York: Norton, 2005), 47.

Chapter 3: The Longing for What Used to Be

1. Sue Monk Kidd, *The Mermaid Chair* (New York: Penguin, 2005).

2. Warren W. Wiersbe, *The Wiersbe Bible Commentary: Old Testament* (Colorado Springs: David C. Cooke, 2007), 524.

Chapter 4: The Longing for Control

1. Thomas à Kempis, *The Imitation of Christ* (Brookfield, IL: Letcetera Publishing, 2015).
2. Walter Scott, *Scott's Poetical Works: Marmion* (London: Adam & Charles Black, 1896), 228. (Canto VI, Stanza XVII)

Chapter 5: The Longing for Your Rights

1. J. R. R. Tolkien, *The Fellowship of the Ring* (New York: Houghton Mifflin, 1994), 58.
2. The Andrew Chan quotes in this chapter are from Chris Makin, "Following Jesus on Death Row," Bible Society, August 3, 2013, http://www.biblesociety.org.au/news/following-jesus-on-death-row.

Chapter 6: The Longing for That One Thing You Think You Need to Be Happy

1. Personal e-mail to the author, permission granted.
2. "The Eagle and the Wolf," Inspirational Christian Stories and Poems website, accessed July 21, 2015, http://www.inspirationalarchive.com/1376/the-eagle-and-the-wolf/.
3. Charles R. Swindoll, *David: A Man of Passion and Destiny* (Nashville: W Publishing Group, 2000), 299.
4. Dietrich Bonhoeffer, *Temptation* (New York: Macmillan, 1935), 116–17.

Chapter 7: The Longing to Make Everything Right

1. Sir Walter Scott, *The Complete Works of Sir Walter Scott, Vol. II* (New York: Conner & Cooke, 1833), 49.
2. Alan Redpath, *The Making of a Man of God* (Grand Rapids, MI: Revell, 1962), 241.

Chapter 8: The Longing for What Would Glorify God

1. Charles Dickens, *David Copperfield* (Orchard Park, NY: Broadview Press, 2001), 405.

2. John W. Lawrence, *Life's Choices* (Portland: Multnomah, 1975), 39.

3. Gene Edwards, *A Tale of Three Kings* (Wheaton, IL: Tyndale, 1980), 98.

Chapter 9: The Longing to Share the Grace and Mercy We've Received from God

1. Anugrah Kumar, "Brennan Manning, Author of 'The Ragamuffin Gospel,' Passes Away," *CP Post*, April 14, 2013, http://www.christianpost.com/news /brennan-manning-author-of-the-ragamuffin-gospel-passes-away-93895/.

2. Augustus M. Toplady, "Rock of Ages, Cleft for Me," verse 3. Music by Thomas Hastings. Public domain.

3. Charles R. Swindoll, *David: A Man of Passion and Destiny* (Nashville: W Publishing Group, 2000), 289.

4. Ian Maclaren, *Beside the Bonnie Brier Bush*, repr. (n.p.: Hard Press, 2006), 64–65, 62–63.

5. Ibid., 66.

Chapter 10: The Longing for God Alone

1. Miguel de Unamuno, *Tragic Sense of Life*, trans. J. E. Crawford Flitch (n.p.: SophiaOmni Press, 2014), 145.

2. Bruce Marshall, *The World, The Flesh and Father Smith*, book club ed. (New York: Houghton Mifflin, 1945), 108.

3. Augustine, *The Confessions of Saint Augustine*, book 1.

4. Pew Research Center, " 'Nones' on the Rise," October 9, 2012, Pew Forum, http://www.pewforum.org/2012/10/09/nones-on-the-rise/.

5. William Barclay, *The Gospel of Luke*, rev. upd. ed. (Louisville: Westminster John Knox, 2001), 236.

6. Ibid., 236–37.

7. Ibid., 237.

8. Elizabeth Cecelia Douglas Clephane, "The Ninety and Nine," lyrics at HymnTime.com, http://www.hymntime.com/tch/pdf/n/i/n/The%20Ninety %20and%20Nine.pdf. Public domain.

9. Karl A. Olsson, *Come to the Party* (Waco, TX: Word, 1972), 19.

10. J. D. Salinger, *The Catcher in the Rye* (New York: Bantam, 1969), 99.

ABOUT THE AUTHOR

SHEILA WALSH IS A POWERFUL COMMUNICATOR, Bible teacher, and bestselling author with more than 5 million books sold. A keynote speaker with Women of Faith for twenty years, Sheila has reached more than 5 million women by combining honesty, vulnerability, and humor with God's Word.

She is the author of *The Storm Inside* and *Loved Back to Life*, and the Gold Medallion nominee for *The Heartache No One Sees*. The Gigi, God's Little Princess book and video series has won the National Retailer's Choice Award twice and is the most popular Christian brand for young girls in the United States. Sheila cohosted *The 700 Club* and her own show *Heart to Heart with Sheila Walsh*.

Twitter: @SheilaWalsh

Facebook: facebook.com/sheilawalshconnects

Instagram: Sheilawalsh1

Do Your Longings Have You Going Around in Circles?

You vowed to never repeat the same mistakes, yet here you are again, right where you started. What is it that keeps drawing you back? In this six-session video-based study, Sheila Walsh shows it is our longings that often lead us into such traps. She draws on her own experiences and the life of King David to reveal that all our longings are rooted in a need for God—and nothing else will satisfy when it comes to filling that void.